# LIFE
# WITH THE
# PANIC
# MONSTER

# LIFE
# WITH THE
# PANIC
# MONSTER

*a guide for the terrified*

## Evelyn Barkley Stewart

Thom Rutledge Publishing ◆ Nashville, Tennessee

## Acknowledgments

*Special thanks to Rick Shelton, Denise Davis, Carol Hamilton, Tonya and Missy, Sidney Bundy, Thom Rutledge, Serenity Peterson, Reggie Anderson. And to my family — Sandra Dalton, sisters Louise and Doris, my parents, and nephews Gabe and Nathan — for being hardheaded, challenging, delightfully "non-mainstream," and totally loving.*

*Finally, thanks to my husband, Maxey, for a shot at the near-perfect marriage award. I'm sure we made the short list.*

Typesetting by Mike Walker, Limbic Graphics, Nashville, Tennessee.
Printing by Vaughn Printing, Inc., Nashville, Tennessee.
Cover Design by Louise Stewart.
Author's Photograph by Doris Stewart.

*For Maxey*

# Table Of Contents

Foreword . . . . . . . . . . . . . . . . . . . . . . . . . . . . . 9

Introduction . . . . . . . . . . . . . . . . . . . . . . . . . 15

## PART ONE: MELTDOWN . . . . . . . . . . . . . . . 19

Chapter 1 . . . . . . . . . . . . . . . . . . . . . . . . . 21

Chapter 2 . . . . . . . . . . . . . . . . . . . . . . . . . 33

Chapter 3 . . . . . . . . . . . . . . . . . . . . . . . . . 51

## PART TWO: RESURGENCE . . . . . . . . . . . . . 61

Chapter 4 . . . . . . . . . . . . . . . . . . . . . . . . . 63

Chapter 5 . . . . . . . . . . . . . . . . . . . . . . . . . 75

Chapter 6 . . . . . . . . . . . . . . . . . . . . . . . . . 87

Chapter 7 . . . . . . . . . . . . . . . . . . . . . . . . . 99

Chapter 8 . . . . . . . . . . . . . . . . . . . . . . . . . 109

Chapter 9 . . . . . . . . . . . . . . . . . . . . . . . . . 123

Chapter 10 . . . . . . . . . . . . . . . . . . . . . . . . 133

Appendix . . . . . . . . . . . . . . . . . . . . . . . . . 139

# Foreword

A panic attack comes suddenly, usually with little or no warning. Within a few moments, there is a shortness of breath, rapid heart beat, shaking, sweating, tightness in the chest, dizziness, and a sense of unreality. It is no wonder that most people who have these experiences believe that they are at the brink of insanity or death. A panic attack is unlike any other event in life. In fact, it is often the defining experience of a person's life.

You hold in your hands the story of one of those lives. The medical profession is learning more and more about effective treatment for panic disorder, but there is no substitute for the support of others who have been there. This is especially true since one of the hallmarks of panic disorder is an ever increasing sense of isolation. *Life with The Panic Monster,* to borrow one of the author's metaphors, is a valuable message in a bottle to those of you who know the monster. I believe that it will prove just as valuable for anyone struggling to understand and support a loved one who has panic attacks, and for health professionals who, whether they know it or not, will at one time or another be treating patients who have panic disorder.

I will leave the story-telling to Evelyn. What follows is the dry stuff: the official definition of panic disorder, along with a brief summary of what we in the medical and the psychiatric community know about it, its consequences, and its treatment. You may want to begin here, or you may want to skip over this information for now and return to it later.

## Definition and Consequences

According to the *Diagnostic and Statistical Manual* of the American Psychiatric Association, panic disorder is characterized by anxiety attacks coupled with worries or fears. Patients commonly experience anxieties about having more attacks, the implications of the current attack, and/or specific concerns about having a debilitating (or fatal) physical illness.

Panic disorder is usually an evolving condition. Most affected persons will initially go to a hospital emergency room or physician for help. If the attacks occur repeatedly, their lives become increasingly restricted. They will avoid places where panic attacks have happened. Then, as the fears build, they will progressively avoid places and situations where escape might be difficult, or help not available if panic occurs. Eventually extensive and generalized phobic avoidance, known as agoraphobia, results.

A panic attack is a disabling experience. Many people with panic disorder suffer impairments in their abilities to travel alone, sometimes even short distances. Sometimes a walk down the block or to the mailbox becomes impossible. The majority lose income, career advancement or even their jobs. They have difficulty with other role responsibilities such as being a parent, spouse or friend. About 40% will have a severe depression during their lives. Seven percent die by suicide.

These problems are not chosen. They are the understandable result of the repeated traumatic experiences of panic attacks. The ramifications of panic disorder as a disabling condition make sense; the consequences would occur to anyone with a similar set of experiences.

## Prevalence and Treatment

This problem affects one to three percent of the population — 2.5 to 7.5 million people in the U.S. As such, it is a huge public health problem. Panic disorder typically begins between the mid-twenties and the late thirties, though panic attacks can occur in children. If untreated, it will become a chronic, life-impairing condition. The longer effective treatment is delayed, the more disability will occur and the more difficult it will be to treat.

If the illness is diagnosed early, most people can be treated quickly. Once it becomes established, it may take months or even years to correct. Many patients experience at least some degree of disability chronically. It is clear that early, aggressive intervention is needed to stem the progression of panic disorder.

The good news is that panic disorder is a treatable condition in the vast majority of people. In our clinic we have found that 90% of our patients either get beyond the condition or experience significant improvement. Treatment, however, remains controversial.

We believe that research supports the effectiveness of both medication and cognitive-behavioral psychotherapy. In fact, it appears that a combination of these two treatments may work best in most people. The medications that have been found to be effective for panic disorder include certain of the antidepressant drugs (whether or not there is a coexisting depression) or two anti-anxiety medicines: alprazolam (Xanax™) or clonazepam (Klonipin™).

There are advantages and disadvantages to the use of these medications. Antidepressant drugs like imipramine (Tofranil™), nortriptyline (Pamelor™), or fluoxetine (Prozac™), among others, have been established as effective anti-panic agents. However, they often cause significant side effects at the beginning of treatment. Although these side effects are most often not dangerous, and do get better or disappear in time, they make treatment initially difficult. In contrast,

Xanax or Klonipin are usually much easier to start. But these medications produce physical dependence if used regularly for more than three months; therefore they are often difficult to discontinue after extended use. There are good reasons for using these medications, however. Bottom line: proper treatment with these medications requires the judgment of a knowledgeable and experienced physician.

## Of Mind and Body

Although medicines are usually effective in blocking panic attacks, they usually do little for the fears and avoidance behavior that accompany the panic. These require more purely psychological interventions to improve in the majority of patients. We have found that cognitive-behavioral therapy is the most effective intervention. This kind of treatment recognizes that a core problem in the condition is a fear of body sensations. People with this disorder will misinterpret relatively mild physical cues (such as an increase in heart rate or shortness of breath) in catastrophic ways. They will fear that these minor physical changes indicate that a serious problem (such as a heart attack) is impending. This psychological event will drive the anxiety even higher, producing a panic attack. Cognitive therapy works by helping patients to identify their fears and learn to correctly interpret their physical sensations. Once the fear is dispelled, the panic will usually diminish.

Ultimately I believe that panic disorder is physiologically based. Recent research, including that in our clinic, has implicated a group of structures deep in the brain that monitor and regulate a critical group of physiological functions, including breathing and heart rate. Panic attacks appear to be a result of an incorrect discharge of brain chemicals that are usually released only at times of extreme distress. In simple terms, the brain is reacting as though a crisis is occurring even though it is not. This release of brain transmitter substances produces the panic response. Current research is investigating possible regulators of this reaction. Substances in the brain that have been implicated include the chemicals serotonin and cholecystokinin. Research in the near future is likely to give us further insight into the cause as well as potential new treatments for panic disorder.

It has been my privilege over many years to treat people with this terrifying condition. I have found them to be remarkably brave and resilient. I have been with them during their struggles and their triumphs, and it has been my joy to be able to work with them. One of these remarkable people is Evelyn Barkley Stewart. I invite you to share in her story.

*Richard C. Shelton, M.D.*
Associate Professor
Department of Psychiatry and Pharmacology
Vanderbilt University School of Medicine

# *Introduction*

This is probably not the book you expect it to be. It's not the book I expected it to be, either. In fact, I didn't even know it was in me until it began fighting for life.

Here is what it's not: a medical book, a scientific study, words to live by, the answer to your problems.

What follows are the notes of a semi-normal woman living with a disorder that wasn't even named until the late seventies. It's a chunk of my life, messy, disorganized, the kinds of things you might confide to a stranger on a long bus trip late into the night, knowing you'd never see them again, dreading the dawn.

I do have a purpose: there are people suffering and in great despair because they have no idea what is wrong with them. And having been one of those walking wounded, I was forced to learn a lot of stuff the hard way.

You know how it is when you want to buy a Volkswagen and suddenly you see Volkswagens everywhere? All at once I started meeting women who had panic disorder and who didn't have a clue about what to do. This book is, among other things, about what to do. I wouldn't presume to call it the light at the end of the tunnel. It's more like a guided tour of the tunnel so you don't have to feel your way through in the dark, alone.

I tried hard to avoid writing this book. Panic disorder is not something you want to chat about in your yearly Christmas letter. ("Ralph was graduated with honors from his small-engine repair home study program, and Evelyn can almost walk to the mailbox alone now.")

This book drove me nuts. I'd go for weeks without writing a word, and then, bam! I'd sit for three hours, scribbling furiously, with a cat on my lap and Tostitos in my free hand.

I do describe in detail the medications I took, which some say is not a good practice. Here is the disclaimer: kids, don't try this at home. If you think you need medication, talk with your doctor, find out what works best for you. This is not one size fits all. It's hard work, but it was harder before. The difference is that this time you have hope.

And in the end, that is my fondest wish for you: I wish you hope.

*E.B.S.*
*January, 1996*

*I am forty years old. I am in a shopping mall in Chattanooga, sitting in a shoe store trying on boots. I bend over to tie the laces, and as I straighten up, my heart begins racing. I feel an explosion of fear in my solar plexus, feel it rush throughout my body. My arms and legs tingle: I can't get my breath. I jerk the boot off and slip into my shoe. I must get out of this store, out of this mall. I leave the store, unable to focus, colors and noises swirling all around me. The walk to the car seems neverending. I sit down, stunned, terrified, believing I am having a heart attack. I am alone one hundred and twenty-five miles from home and gasping for air. I try to think rationally, but my body has gone beyond my conscious control. It is too late for technique. All I can do is hang on for dear life, ride this out, wait to see if I die.*

*I begin to drive. On the interstate huge trucks are passing me. I feel like I will faint at any moment. I believe if I pull over and stop, a trucker will find me dead in my car.*

*I grasp the steering wheel, I try to breathe, I pray to live. I think I will never see my husband again, and I start to cry. Today is our wedding anniversary.*

*A life lived in fear.*

# PART ONE:

# MELTDOWN

*"I began to see things as they ain't."*

*— line from "Hard-Hearted Hannah,
the Vamp of Savannah"*

# Chapter 1

There is a reason why we begin our stories recounting our very first panic attack: with it comes a clear message that life as we have known it will never be the same. It is an earth-shattering event, and if you listen closely you can hear the fabric of your life split apart. And in that instant you are swept through the rent into a place where danger waits at every turn, where terror strikes as unexpectedly as lightning on a clear day, where our closest and most constant companion is fear.

I was in my twenty-ninth year of life and first year of marriage when I tumbled down Alice's rabbit hole into that other place. Here is the setup: My husband Maxey and I were living in an apartment in Chattanooga, and we decided it was time to buy our first home. We called a realtor and invited her over to educate us, which, in retrospect, was a little like begging an Amway representative to please come make a presentation.

For more than two hours she sat and discussed amortization and balloon payments and thirty years' worth of debt. My eyes were glazed and I feared my facial expression of feigned interest would become fixed and permanent. I think I served snacks.

After a couple of lifetimes she stood and we three began the half-hearted shuffle to the door, and then it happened. Suddenly I felt dizzy. The room veered crazily. I reached out to touch the wall for balance and reassurance, but got neither. Amazingly I managed to stay upright, smiling graciously, ushering the Realtor from Hell out the door, without attracting attention to my condition. As the latch clicked behind her, I dropped down on all fours and lowered my head to the floor. My husband was astounded. All I could say was, "I'm so dizzy," over and over.

I was terrified. My senses had been stolen from me, and for no apparent reason.

After several minutes the dizziness began to pass, and though I regained my composure, the fear lingered. After all these years that feeling is as familiar to me as the palm of my hand. But on an evening in 1978 it was brand new, an unknown entity, large enough to over-shadow my whole life. I know now it was my first encounter with the power of the panic monster.

From this safe distance it is so easy to see that given the situation, a panic attack was practically unavoidable. I had moved away from the safety of family and friends. I was adjusting to marriage. I was asking to take on the largest financial debt I could imagine and finally, I had sat too long, tense and anxious. It's so *obvious.* And yet at the time, I could come up with no other explanation than some serious malfunction of my body, like a brain tumor. It set the tone for the next eleven years.

Five years prior I had completed my training as a clinical social worker, which makes this more embarrassing. I was good at my work, could assess other people's problems, but when it came to my own situation I was completely baffled. Clinician, heal thyself.

At the time of this first attack I was working on a women's unit at the state mental institute. Believe me, the irony was not lost on me. I was the social worker on a twenty-five bed unit. Our psychiatrist was a portly Englishman who smoked cigarettes constantly and wrote stories about his adventures in North Africa during World War II.

The women assigned to our unit were of all ages with problems of every sort. Some I came to know well because they returned to the unit again and again. It's a familiar pattern: they would come in hallucinating, delusional, whatever; get regulated on their medication; leave the hospital and immediately stop taking the medicine; and reappear at our door within one to six months. It was fairly routine.

There was one woman I have never forgotten. Ava was somewhere between twenty-five and forty, had lank brown hair that lay flat against her head and fell to her shoulders. She wore dark-framed cat's eyes glasses and turquoise double knit slacks that were a couple of sizes too large. Talk about your fashion suicide. Fact is, no one really noticed. The unit dress code for patients appeared to be 60's Tacky Party.

Anyway, Ava spent every waking hour going from one person to the next, staff and patients alike, plucking at sleeves, shifting constantly from one foot to the other in a kind of Thorazine shuffle, her voice breathy with fear, asking over and over: "Am I going to die today? Am I?" And we, the highly professional staff, gave the usual range of answers from, "No, Ava," to "We all will die some day, but probably not today." So reassuring.

Once someone thought to ask Ava why she was so worried about dying, and she replied that she had committed the Unpardonable Sin and was terrified of dying and being put into a coffin. Furthermore, she could not tell us what the Unpardonable Sin was, exactly, which may have caused some of the staff (not me certainly) to examine their lives in the privacy of their own homes.

Ava was brought to our unit many times for treatment. One morning I arrived at work to find Ava gone, AMA. It seems she flew the coop with the wizened little cabdriver who always brought her in.

We celebrated her daring escape as a small triumph over her fear, no matter how unlikely the love match might have seemed to us.

Over these years I have thought of her often: Am I going to die today, Ava? Am I?

---

Several months after my initial attack my symptoms persisted: I had dizzy spells, my heart raced, I felt separated from things around me. I was guarded and ill at ease a lot of the time. I suspected all sorts of culprits: multiple sclerosis, a brain tumor, blood clots, insanity, all kinds of dire diagnoses. I used to worry that I had Hodgkin's Disease until the cure rate went over 80%. I scoured drug store shelves for magazines with articles entitled "The Hidden Disease" and "Could *You* Be Suffering From..." and my answer was — well, yes, I *could* be. But in the dead of night when rationality has fled, my answer was Oh God, I *know* I've got it! After lo these many years I understand that I was suffering from anticipatory anxiety, fear of fear. Back then it never occurred to me that there was an answer other than physical illness. Fear was not an acceptable alternative. Fear was something you could control, not vice versa. Right?

So I started keeping track of my body, believing (wrongly) that any action was better than immobility. Secretly I monitored my heartbeat, took my temperature, checked the whites of my eyes for signs of jaundice and my nail beds for the telltale blue of insufficient oxygen. It was humiliating, and I couldn't stop. I thought if I were not constantly vigilant, something terrible would happen. Of course it happened anyway, it happened *because* of my vigilance. The worst part was that mentally, logically, I knew these fears were irrational, but knowing that was no protection from the panic monster. I was easy pickings.

Where do you start? With a doctor, of course. My supervisor at work gave me the name of her internist. I made an appointment and prayed to the great god Hippocrates for an easy cure.

I arrived at the doctor's office to find the waiting room hot, overcrowded, and furnished in the unmistakable decor of the 1950's: pole lamps and orange plastic molded chairs which were bolted to the floor. In addition to being bolted to the floor, each chair was attached to every other chair in the row, reminiscent of a chain gang. I sat down to wait my turn and made myself as small as possible.

The scent of plastic coupled with that of scores of would-be patients proved too much for me. I was horrified to feel a panic attack coming on. Pure fear propelled me through a sea of humanity to the front window, where I told a nurse I was going to faint. She took me to a small room with an examining table where I could lie down and panic in private.

The doctor was a short, kindly, white-haired man of about fifty who came in and did what doctors do: he thumped me, peered into all orifices above the neck, listened to my heart. I was pronounced allergic. "Your throat looks like Niagara Falls," he declared. He gave me a painful shot, antihistamines to go, kissed me on the forehead, and sent me on my way. We both were thrilled that he had pinned the tail on my elusive donkey on the first try.

By my third visit we both knew my sinuses had let us down. His disappointment was thinly veiled as he gave me the name of an ear, nose, and throat man. A specialist. It had begun.

The ENT guy was young and energetic and offered me the opportunity of taking a test which consisted of pouring water into my ears at intervals over a period of hours, to measure-what? Endurance? Stupidity? In my heart of hearts I knew there was nothing remarkable about my ears. I said thanks, but no thanks, and in this game of medical tag, he got me last: he referred me to a neurologist.

Now remember, I had worked in a medical hospital. My fear of neurologists was almost as great as my panic. Here was a man who could actually confirm, after multiple painful tests involving needles and electricity, that I indeed had a brain tumor with a side order of MS as a special bonus (not available in stores!). I asked my husband to drive me to my appointment, not only for support, but so he could take me to the hospital for the inevitable "admission for testing." Read: torture.

This neurologist, busy as he was, took a *full ten minutes* to assess my case. He had me close my eyes, extend my arms, and touch my nose. He had me hold both arms side by side at shoulder height, again with eyes closed. (I can't tell you how useful these little exercises have been to me over the years to rule out my periodic brain tumors.) He asked me how things were going at work. I can't remember what I said. Then he handed me a prescription for Valium, 5 mg. as needed, up to four times daily. Relief and embarrassment fought mightily for supremacy. On the one hand, I wasn't dying of anything. On the other, these terrible symptoms were nothing more than "in my head." How could this be? I took a Valium and forgot the question.

So for the next three years I lived and worked in Chattanooga. It's a tough town to break into unless you were born there, live on a mountain, or best of all possible worlds, were born on a mountain. The main export may have been polyester. Finally I was able to make a couple of good friends who have stood the test of time and distance, but for the most part, I spent many nights alone. With Maxey's job, often I was headed for my morning shower as he was just getting in from work.

During those years my full-blown panic attacks were relatively rare. I had more of a sense of dis-ease, a feeling of not fitting in, a fairly constant tension just getting by. My dark brown hair started to turn white. I was gradually losing weight. I look at old photographs and see the fear behind the smile, the self-conscious posturing. I felt threatened from within and without.

In my journal I wrote: "I get the sweats, the shakes, the fear — that oppressive, impending doom feeling. I was fine until I tried to sleep and had that horrible feeling I was leaving my body. My balance is shot again..." and on and on. I was so weary of focusing on myself, but I truly believed if I stopped I would not survive. I was too ashamed to tell anyone about these feelings. So I ended up doing what most of us do — going to the doctor for symptoms I still believed — feared — were physical in origin. The reassurance usually lasted nearly twenty-four hours.

I kept on taking the Valium, but it certainly was not the panacea we all used to believe. It did keep me upright and moving as opposed to supine and immobile. It did allow me to continue to be at large. And then we all read *I'm Dancing As Fast As I Can* and I even became afraid of the Valium. I was fast running out of escape routes.

One of the various ways panic disorder affects us is that gradually it erodes our judgment. We have cried wolf so often we hesitate to present symptoms for fear we will get that look — you know the one I mean. The "not again, deep sigh" response. We begin to believe that everything we feel is a byproduct of our fear, or at least that this is how others perceive it. And so it happened that one night when Maxey was out of town, after a chili supper and roller skating,

I came home and felt ill. I was awake all night in pain, but I stayed calm. The next morning I called in to work and happened to speak to one of the doctors. When I offhandedly described the ache in my side, she sent someone to take me to the hospital. I was not afraid even when the appendicitis was diagnosed and sailed through the surgery and hospital stay. But I distinctly remember two days after I came home staring at my red and swollen forearm where the IV had irritated the vein, positive I had developed an embolism which would travel to my brain and damage me beyond repair. I don't know how Maxey stood it. I could hardly stand myself. I could no longer distinguish between real and imagined danger when my own body was involved.

Meanwhile back at the institute I had been promoted to Director of Admissions. This meant I was the first stop for patients hot off the streets, arriving in varying degrees of compliance. Some strolled in on their own; some were brought in handcuffed and shackled by police. Every day held the promise of adventure.

One morning I looked up from my desk to find a dwarf, barefooted, dressed only in bloodstained pajamas, escorted by officers of the law. He was calm and matter-of-fact as he told his story. It seems he lived with an elderly aunt, who had awakened to find him standing at the foot of her bed in the early morning hours.

There was some confusion at this point concerning his attire, which may have been none at all, but we let that slide. In her fright she bounded out of bed, ran down the stairs and leapt off the front porch, fracturing her hip as she landed in a hedge.

The dwarf attempted to go for help in the car, which recently had been fitted out with hand controls since his feet could not reach the floorboards. Unfortunately for just about everyone, he had not yet received driver's ed. He ended up in the ditch, slightly wounding himself in the process, which accounted for the bloodstains on his pajamas. The police, who believe they have seen it all, found him. I cannot imagine the discussion that ensued, but in the end, through wisdom or bewilderment, they brought him to us.

After listening to the dwarf's account of events, I called in the psychiatrist who had to see all emergency admissions. His name was Dr. Nallamothu, and was as darkly handsome as Omar Sharif. With one look he took in the dwarf, his stained pajamas, his bare feet and in his clipped Indian accent said: "What happened to you?" "Aw Doc," the dwarf replied, "I was born this way."

---

Irrational terror is stigmatizing, and is nearly impossible to explain to someone who has never experienced it. Recently I refused a drink, and when pressed (as often people do) I told the man I had panic disorder and couldn't drink alcohol. A little while later in the evening he said to me, "I still like you in spite of that thing you get."

Please understand that this is a man who makes a fortune buying and selling companies and is a graduate of West Point.

This is why we become so skillful at keeping our secret: fear is not an acceptable disease. My nervous system, or brain chemicals, misfire from time to time, for whatever reason, and it's no one's fault, not even mine. Theories abound about what causes panic disorder, and there are even more treatments, which range from daily analysis to lining your hat with aluminum foil. But I'm getting ahead of myself. Treatment comes later.

What the hell, Doc: I was born this way.

# Chapter 2

When I was fifteen years old I flew in an airplane for the first time. It was a prop plane, and I flew from my grandparents' home in Alabama to Knoxville, Tennessee, all by myself. I clearly remember watching the runway rushing by, certain the plane would never leave the ground. When it finally did, I was thrilled and enchanted, and stared wide-eyed out the window the whole trip. I felt very grown up.

Three years ago I had to fly from Nashville to Washington, alone. I dreaded the trip for days, even had a near fainting spell in the shower the day before I left. Once on the plane, I was quietly terror-stricken, listening for some flaw in the roar of the engines, watching the wing flap up and down like it would snap off any second. Luckily, I wound up with one of those seatmates who is so incredibly boring and self-involved that a plane crash could have been a welcome interruption.

What had changed? The air was the same, as was the earth below, but I was different. Twenty-eight years later, and I did not feel grown up in the least. I wanted someone to hold my hand. I wanted the impossible: the promise that I would not die in a fiery plane crash, or in the shower with the water beating down on me, or in a lunch meeting, my face falling into my plate. I want a guarantee. This is a problem. The closest I can get is that like we told Ava, the odds are against me dying at this particular moment. Not good enough for people who panic. Our worst fear is loss of control, and to me, death represents the ultimate and complete loss of the illusion of control we cling to so tenuously.

It is curious to me that others seem to lack this fear of death. What are they thinking? I'd like to believe they are so busy leading rich and rewarding lives that they don't contemplate dying. But I can't. Here's what I believe: that they are out there pretending the knock will never come at their door. That the one who gets cancer is someone their cousin knows. The parent of a friend. Their sister-in-law's hairdresser. They read about a death in the newspaper. For a moment they gaze into space — and then the curtain is drawn again.

Here's who dies: My mother, my grandparents, my cousins, two great aunts, two young nephews, two close friends, five friends from college. There will be more.

And here's how it happens: it's a cosmic game of Drop the Handkerchief. We all stand in a circle holding hands while death circles around and around behind us. We hear the footsteps stop. Then we watch while the light leaves the eyes of someone we love. We throw handfuls of dirt on a box in a hole in the ground. Do you get it? Am I the only one who doesn't get it?

One difference between those who panic and those who don't is that we have been forced to see that control is an illusion. Our struggle is about learning to live comfortably with that fact.

———

After three years of living in Chattanooga, Maxey was transferred to Nashville. For six months he made a weekly commute to Nashville that began on Monday mornings and ended on Thursday nights. Faced with the prospect of moving, Chattanooga started looking like the Promised Land, and I did everything I could to drag my feet concerning the move.

It was inevitable. I had the standard awkward farewell lunch with co-workers. Maxey and I spent weekends in Nashville, looking at houses.

We were lucky. We found a wonderful house in a small town twenty miles outside Nashville. It was a house in the woods, secluded but accessible, safe for our cats and dog, safe for me, I hoped against hope.

The actual move defies my poor powers of description. Maxey was already in Nashville, on the job. The movers packed up everything, so I spent my last night in a totally empty house. Early the next morning I witnessed the divorce of a dear friend, ate breakfast, and took off for my new home with two cats in a loaded down car. One cat was so carsick that she sat on my shoulder and actually projectile vomited onto the passenger side window. I got lost in downtown Nashville and by the time I stopped for directions the man I asked laughed out loud.

Some hours later when I arrived at the house I found it deserted except for the sea of boxes the movers had been paid to unpack. In the absence of an authority figure, they scrammed. When Maxey came home he was able to locate me by following the sound of my sobbing. He was less than ecstatic (far, far less) when I wailed that I wanted to go home. I'll say it: I don't travel well. I am not a good sport when uprooted.

This was in the spring of 1981. I have delayed for days writing about the next few years. The events were intensely painful and difficult to reconstruct. I kept journals throughout these years, which undoubtedly kept me relatively sane, but re-reading them resurrects those ghosts, calls them up, gives them new life. I have to stop and separate that past from my present. Back then I was drowning in my fears, bailing out my sinking boat with a sieve.

I left Chattanooga on a Friday and began my new job with the Department of Mental Health in downtown Nashville the following Monday. I worked there for eleven months. I honestly don't have the remotest idea what I did there, but whatever it was, it was done on strict schedule, every moment accounted for in writing at the end of the day. This job was administrative, and all my education and experience was in clinical social work. Counseling. Direct services. Face to face stuff.

Let me quickly say (before someone else volunteers) that I am terrible at administrative work. I am seated at a desk, handed a budget, or a grant proposal, or God forbid, the Federal Register. My eyes instantly glaze over and I lose the ability to comprehend what has been set before me. This happened repeatedly for nearly one year. I was in over my head, and no matter what I did, I could not touch bottom. Imagine: a person with undiagnosed panic disorder, in a strange city, in a job where everybody but her knows the language and the customs.

I sat through endless useless meetings, trying to pass for normal, desperate to fit in, and failing miserably. I perfected the look of the deer caught in the headlights of an official state car. I tried to pay attention in the meetings, but invariably I'd begin to see spots, or feel my body begin to tingle, or my heart begin to beat so heavily I was sure it showed through my blouse. I was frightened, to a greater or lesser extent, hypervigilant, nearly all the time. Lunch meetings were absolute hell, because I had to try to eat while I was scared. In nature this does not occur and for good reason: food cannot be digested when your heart is in your throat.

I couldn't seem to find a place where I could relax, let my guard down, just be myself. Everything felt like a test. I came home from work, stared at the television, fell into bed. Weekends we cleaned house. And the single thread that ran throughout was guilt: it was all my fault.

My big break came when a friend told me of a job opening for a hospital social service director. It sounded great. I applied, and got the job. A week before I was to begin work I discovered I was pregnant. This was in April, 1982. It turned out to be a bigger break than I expected.

---

It still amazes me that during these years I was able to dress myself, go to work, and live in such a way that I appeared to be a normal, functioning person, while just below the surface, waves rose and fell, tides rolled in and out, the earth trembled, and nothing felt solid. Periodically the panic broke through full force, convincing me that something was wrong with me physically. I monitored all my bodily goings-on with alacrity, translating the most harmless symptoms into dread diseases. I came to think of the fear as a monster who lived in some deep recess in me and attacked at random. I felt vulnerable and unprotected. My fear finally began to *produce* physical symptoms, which more or less closed the circle. Perfect: I had succeeded in creating a life cycle for the panic monster which could be repeated endlessly. I remember wondering one fall if I would live until Christmas.

The day before I was to begin my job at the hospital I began to bleed. I had to call my new boss and tell him that I was pregnant, but not for long. He was sympathetic. We delayed my starting date for one week.

On Monday I miscarried while I was at my new gynecologist's office. I rode home in shock. I wanted a baby desperately, and had come so close, just to watch it slip away, all within a matter of a few days. People said: At least now you know you can get pregnant, and especially, It was *meant* to be lost. As if this would cheer me up. I wanted to beat them senseless. If you ever start a consolation speech with "at least," you'd better duck.

The following day I was still having some pain, so the doc sent me across the street to the hospital for a D&C. For several hours I waited in a windowless room with cinderblock walls. When the phlebotomist had to search for a vein for the IV, I became hysterical. Maxey told me later people in the hallway outside could hear me. He knew this because he was in the hallway outside. Who could blame him? I was as close to crazy and out of control as I never hope to be. I truly believed I would not wake up after the surgery.

But I did, and we rode home in silence, and I sat on the floor in front of the bedroom window and cried. What else is there? I had to pull myself together for this swell new job, so I got my hair cut. That's what women do when there's no grave to put flowers on. We cut our hair, or color it, or get a new bedspread. We always find a way to mark the occasion, in secret.

---

### *A LETTER TO MY SISTER*

Dear Weezie —

I got the job at the hospital. (Be careful what you wish for). I spent the whole first two weeks meeting department heads, trying (and failing, I fear) to be charming a week after the miscarriage and I don't have any clothes to wear. I need professional looking suits and blouses — read dowdy. Send me anything you can't wear any more. Or even if you can.

---

I've got this staff of nine who doubt my competence and challenge my authority. Perfect. It's not like I'm teeming with self-confidence at this point. I was hoping for a place where I could feel useful and like I belonged. What I've stepped into is a veritable mine field of secret angers and hidden agendas, and I manage to stumble around blindly and set off one or two a day. I feel like a stepmother, saying all the wrong things. The parts of me I offer up are refused and rebuffed. What this staff wants is clearly unclear and most likely an item I don't carry. I take a Valium every morning. The truth is I could stroll these hospital halls with a Valium IV drip in one arm and a drink in my free hand and still be tense. My wants are few: I want the staff to like me, and for them to do their jobs. Silly me. These are people in the helping professions. Educated people. You know: crybabies.

Not much good news I'm afraid. Maxey tries to help but is so caught up in his own problems. We both look like hell. I'm thinking of seeing a therapist for a second opinion. I don't trust my own right now.

*Enough about me. So how's bayou? And the new business venture? Are you seeing anybody? Tell me all. I desperately need some vicarious thrills. Miss you. Kiss the boys for me —*

*XX*

*Evie*

*P.S.- Don't forget the clothes. And don't try to slip in any I gave you.*

I stayed at the job for four and a half years. I did take a 5 mg. Valium each morning and countless nights I got out of bed and lay on the bathroom rug, waiting for the intestinal cramps to subside. Every day I went to work, jaw clenched, ready for fight or flight. I lost weight. My hair turned silver. I developed a slight tremor that I discovered while I was taking photographs.

I tell myself it can't *all* have been that bad. Surely I've just forgotten the good parts. But when I re-read those journals, all I see is pain, fear, separateness. In all fairness I do take responsibility for some of my awful experiences there. These were good people. Some became, and have remained, close friends. You know who you are.

The rest of you can write you own book about what a crummy boss I was.

Why couldn't I quit? Like most of us who live with panic disorder, I thought it was my fault it was not working out, and if I could just figure out how to fix it, everything would be fine. And in the end I was so demoralized and beaten into submission that I couldn't even consider looking for another job.

I kept searching for the answer, and got second, third, and fourth opinions: spastic colon, said my doctor. Low self-esteem, said my therapist. Wrong job for you, said my friend. Gotcha, said the panic monster. Repeatedly.

Seeing the therapist didn't fix me, but at least it patched me up enough to keep going. I was never officially diagnosed as having panic disorder, but he tried to help with my fears and a nervous system that was on the long downward slide. We attempted guided meditations and relaxation therapy. Failed miserably. The exercises made me feel like I was losing control, and actually brought on panic.

Back then (of course!) I just thought I wasn't doing it right. I learned a lot about myself, which is good, but it didn't lessen my fear. ("Knowledge is power," he said, and I was impressed. Days later I heard it on a commercial for kids during Saturday morning cartoons. Or wait. Maybe he said "Knowledge is not power." I forget.) Anyway, I would drive over to see him once a week, have my hour, excuse me;

fifty minutes, and get back in the car where the panic monster was waiting in the passenger seat, playing with the knobs on the radio. "So what did we learn today, little girl? And are you aware that you're late for work?"

It's a miracle that my marriage and I survived those years. Maxey and I loved each other deeply, but were so needy we didn't have a lot left over to give. We were good to each other, considerate, caring. We still could laugh together, which probably was what saved us during the nights when he slept in the spare bedroom or I took to the sofa. We just did the best we could to keep living. Every day I had a new symptom, some different disease. Then, for no reason, I would be panic-free for a while, and think I'd beaten it. And up it would rise and slap me in mid-swagger with a pie-in-the-face routine, and I'd be devastated. Why me? I'd whine and carry on. Nothing personal, the monster would reply, whipping out a brand new symptom, breaking all the rules.

There isn't much more to say about those years before 1986. I depended on my family, a few close friends, and a Valium a day to get me through. I was sick a lot; our cat got killed; I didn't get pregnant. I looked like one of those awful drawings of the children with the big eyes. If I'd seen what was coming, I'd have tried to have eaten more.

I keep putting off beginning this segment. I get up and roam around, looking for something, anything else to do but this. Nothing. Still, I wait. The cat sits in my lap, uses my hand as a salt lick. I look down and see that she's removed a thin layer of skin without me even knowing it. What does she do at night? Sometimes she turns on the radio and also has changed the time the alarm is set to go off. She's practically bilingual.

Enough! It was on May 14, 1986, when I called home to check on some test results my mother had. My father answered. He said they had found some suspicious cells in the fluid taken from my mother's lung. "Adeno cells," he called them. Immediately I phoned her doctor, who had treated her for most of her adult life. In great distress he told me she had lung cancer, and felt personally responsible for not having found it sooner. I told him I was certain he had always given her the best of care, and pressed him for a prognosis. He paused a long time. Poor, he said finally. It's poor.

Within two hours Maxey and I were on the road to Knoxville. Mama had been admitted to the hospital to find out the extent of the cancer. When we arrived, I was able to be alone with her for a few minutes. We hugged each other hard, and cried.

We stayed through the week until she had her first dose of chemotherapy and was discharged. The cancer was confined to the pleural fluid of the lung, if you can call that confined. She felt good and looked as pretty as ever. We headed home, steeped in denial. It's what you do.

When we were very young, my sisters and I, our mother contracted a rare lung disease. Treatment in 1950 was primitive. She had ribs from her back removed, collapsing her left lung, and was isolated from us for eighteen months. It helped shape all three of us. Louise, the eldest at age four, became permanent point man. Doris, age two, withdrew to that place where she believed she would be safe from pain; and I, at age one, was afraid of everything. I don't blame my panic disorder on my early childhood. It's not that. My father somehow managed to keep us together at home, clothed, changed, fed, and loved us, not knowing whether his wife would live or die. But here's the thing: our deepest, darkest fears hardly ever come true, and I found myself staring down the barrel of that particular shotgun. I was thirty-eight years old. I felt ten, and a hundred.

Two weeks later Maxey and I attended high school graduation ceremonies for our nephew, Steven. Maxey's brother videotaped the whole thing, just as he had the week before for his younger son's graduation from eighth grade. After the ceremony Steven came up to me and hugged me, his eyes shining. He said "This is the happiest I've ever been." We went to their home for a big family celebration dinner and smiled as Steven and his girlfriend held hands under the dinner table.

The next morning we were awakened at seven by a phone call. It was Maxey's father. The boys were killed, he said, sometime after midnight, in the car that had been Steven's graduation gift. Steven was driving, missed a turn, and struck a tree. Trent, his brother, was killed outright. Steven died at the hospital. Their cousin Michael was seriously injured. He required months to recuperate from his physical injuries, and both his lifelong best friends were dead.

My parents came to Nashville for the double funeral.

The day after, I wallpapered a room, alone.

That summer was a tribute to the survival instinct. Our lives were shattered, the ground littered with shards of glass. If you tripped you would be cut to ribbons. At work a staff member insisted on a formal meeting with my supervisor so she could present her complaints. We met for an hour and a half. I didn't even defend myself. My boss had to do that for me. It wasn't that I felt responsible for her dissatisfaction. On the contrary, I had little interest in her complaints and even less energy for devising any solutions. She said she was sorry to have to do this at a time like this. I laughed out loud.

The better part of the summer was spent bouncing back and forth between hand-wringing anxiety and paralyzing depression. I was sick frequently, sometimes thought I had colon cancer. I lost a tooth to infection. Almost daily I had some symptom that frightened me, further threatening my already weakened defense system. I was struggling in quicksand.

That summer I had one of my worst panic attacks. I was sitting in the hospital cafeteria, eating lunch with four or five of the staff. We were talking about the recent hospital picnic, and I made a simple remark about one of the administrators. Seven years later I remember it perfectly: "Ted Kelly sure is competitive," I said, and it might as well have been an incantation for the response it brought on. Faster than a speeding bullet, my heart took off, the world dropped away, and I knew I was going to faint. I could not breathe or focus. I said I suddenly was not feeling well, the understatement of perhaps this century, and asked someone to help me back to my office. Once inside, my attack not only did not abate, but took on mammoth proportions. Wave after wave of dizziness broke over me. I called my husband, my therapist, and my doctor, in that order. All I could do was hang on for dear life. There was no place to hide. With the panic monster you are always naked, and in the open.

After about three hours of this torture I was exhausted, resourceless, defenseless. I no longer cared if I died, so naturally the panic ceased. My fire had consumed itself.

In the end there was something incredibly freeing in that experience. My cover was blown. My true identity was revealed . And it was not Wonder Woman. What a relief.

By July Mama had begun losing energy and was weaker. The chemotherapy took most of her hair, and Daddy cut off the few remaining strands that somehow were spared. We made the trip to Knoxville frequently. I saw her become ill and frail. My father cared for her, just as he had for us thirty-five years earlier, totally and lovingly, at home. Sometimes when I called home she would whisper a few words into the phone. Later, when she no longer had the strength to speak, she would mouth the words to my father, who passed them on to me. In July I prayed she would live until Christmas. By August I was praying that she wouldn't have to live through Thanksgiving. It was answered. She died in her bed at home, Daddy by her side, in early September.

After the funeral I returned to work and submitted my resignation. Millay: "O I am grown so free from care since my heart broke!"

# Chapter 3

When I stopped working in October of 1986 I sat down. For the first time in my adult life I just sat and looked out the window. Mornings I got up, opened the bedroom curtains, fixed my cup of hot tea, and sat up in bed with the cats looking out over the pond. It was delightful. I know I needed solitude and rest. I was severely damaged, and didn't care to be around other people. I did begin talking out loud, alone, and enjoyed it. I talked to myself, and quite a bit to my mother. Sometimes I had conversations with the television.

I do remember writing my friend Joan, telling her I had lost faith in everything. Very gradually I did begin to believe again, although from a different perspective. For someone who has never struggled through losses, faith is an easy thing to have, comforting and comfortable as an old shawl. When handsome boys die young,

51

and your mother is put into the earth, the faith you reclaim is blood-stained, as if you dug the graves yourself with bare hands. I wanted to bleed; needed to.

Am I going to die today, Ava, am I? For a time I lost the fear because I no longer cared.

I think the panic monster slept for a while. In the backwash of real tragedy there is no room for an imagined fear. Pain takes up most of the space.

I envisioned my life as a thousand feet deep, and I was living in only the top three feet. I had to protect myself from the monster who lived in the depths. I believed if I lived quietly enough, lived an unremarkable life, he would not awaken.

And of course I was wrong.

Tonight I am nervous, jumpy, alone. I think it is hormonal. I think it is emotional. I think it is my illness. I don't want to tell this story tonight. The monster is rattling his chains, making me unsteady, making me think of MS and brain tumors, like the old days. I hope to God the chains hold. It is, at these times, a most fragile existence.

Where was I? Taking the rest cure. By the spring of 1987 I was feeling guilty about not working. I knew I needed to work to shift my attention away from myself, but social work was out of the question.

That particular account was way overdrawn. So naturally I took a position as manager of a large bookstore. Manager! I had no retail experience, couldn't even run a cash register. Whatever were we thinking?

I was excellent at parts of the job, miserable at others. I did love the books, touching them, stacking them, and I was fairly star-struck when authors came in for signings. The work was endless, physically and mentally exhausting, and after nine months (yes, I see it) the owners and I parted amicably, citing irreconcilable differences.

I don't recall having panic attacks during those nine months. I remember the long drives home, falling into bed at night, sleeping heavily, and starting all over again. I was under pressure from every-where to learn all aspects of the job, beginning with the cash register and ending with the corporation, but in the end it was just one more place where I didn't belong. What I did learn was sticks and stones may break your bones, but retail will pulverize you into a fine powder. And quitting jobs was beginning to get easier.

I stopped work in January of 1988. Unfortunately, the next several months were a long downward slide. My anxiety had come back, and physically I was too tired to fight it. I had lots of those never thoughts: I'll never have a baby, I'll never be well...I was all out of ideas about how to get back on track. And it was not for lack of trying. I'd attended stress management seminars, seen therapists, taken a course in Reike, been to Jazzercise, had my palm read, used the runes, done my color chart, had my aura photographed, held rocks, and lit candles. My panic monster sailed through it all with out a scratch, without a hair out of place. You know the drill: if I squashed one symptom, another popped up, each more frightening and exotic than the last. And with my experience in medical and mental health treatment, I had an endless source of material from which to choose. Spiritually I felt like a tattered rag on a stick.

In my journal I came across a list of fears I had written down. I guess I hoped by cataloging them I could take away some of their power. You will recognize them and may even have some I have not even thought of.

### FEARS

| | |
|---|---|
| Maxey dying | Getting caught for |
| Daddy dying | old mistakes |
| Having an operation | Not getting pregnant |
| Having a brain tumor | Getting pregnant |
| Me dying — alone | Not finding work |
| Aliens coming for me | Taking the wrong job |
| (Courtesy of the book *Communion*) | Getting old |
| Going crazy | Having panic attacks |
| Agoraphobia | Leaving my body |
| Having cancer | Losing my friends |
| Having a stroke | because I'm too needy. |

The shopping list from Hell.

After that I wrote: "Here is the truth (I can't wait to see what this will be): There is nothing wrong with you physically. You are not going crazy. There are no aliens in the bedroom. The truth is you are running from someone, your true self, and there aren't many more places to hide. When you stop running, you will stop being afraid, because you will no longer be pursued."

Wow. For a moment there I must have been channeling some rational dead person.


Recently I learned that a friend of mine has ovarian cancer. She had a hysterectomy and is taking chemotherapy. Her prognosis is good. She plans on living.

When I hear things like this I am ashamed of having terrors about nameless, faceless phantoms I can't point to when others are facing real challenges — diseases with names, with descriptions, with results that not the worst of which may be death. You can't capture the likeness of the panic monster on a CT scan. He's not going to come two-stepping across your screen with a hat and cane. Instead he waits until you are resting comfortably, or involved in some project, or walking to the mailbox, and then he sets off all the fire alarms. You run shrieking, deafened, bumping into yourself searching for an exit. Guess what? He's locked all the doors. And just when you're certain death is imminent, when you can't bear it one moment more, it's over. You're left spent, exhausted, alive, at the edge of the precipice. Always at the edge.

In May of 1988 I found out I was pregnant. In June I miscarried. I was devastated. I knew this was my last chance, and this body blew it. What do you do? It's a death, and you do whatever it is that you do when someone dies. The death of a dream takes a long, long time to heal.

———

Then in August I saw the ad: Social Worker, Part-time, Hospice. I interviewed and took the job on the spot.

Why warm your hands when you can leap into the fire? In the darkest part of me, where no light ever shone, in the lair of the panic monster, lived the deepest terror: death. I wanted a showdown with my fear. I wanted to bring death out of the shadows, immerse myself in it, examine it in the daylight. Be careful what you wish for: in one year I had fifty opportunities.

In my second week of work I was at the home of an elderly patient, sitting in the kitchen with his daughter-in-law, when he just up and died. I felt like Prissy with Melanie's baby coming. But I called our nurse, phoned relatives to inform them, helped the nurse clean up the gentleman and combed his hair. It was important that he look presentable when the family came in to say goodbye. Our gentle ministrations seemed almost like a form of worship, like a sacred thing. I will never forget the experience, especially seeing his arms stretched heavenward, minutes before he died. I wish I could have seen what he saw.

What I learned in that year was something about natural balance. I met death, but I also encountered life. There was plenty of fear, but there was more courage. I saw families call up resources and strengths they never dreamed they possessed. I did the same.

I tried to keep my heart open, knowing the cost would be high. I did it anyway. Some who loved me wanted me to stop the work, didn't want me to have to experience the pain. I couldn't make them understand that working with the dying, and those who love them, is a job that cuts to the bone. It's unambiguous and clean. I was good at it. All I had to do was offer myself up like a buffet, and people could go through and pick out what they needed. Trouble was, sometimes I couldn't replenish myself.

There was a subtle kind of erosion going on. I really believed I was doing okay, though I wrote that my eyes felt like ball bearings. I would have said I felt fine, although I was having headaches and dizzy spells and dreamed one night I was one of triplets. And I had the panic attack at the mall in Chattanooga during this period. Doing great. You know: other than that, Mrs. Lincoln, how did you like the play?

We are coming to the end of the first section. Thank God, you say, and so do I. The treatment years are much more upbeat and fun-filled than the killer years we've just passed through. Only a little more to go. Stay in there with me.

It was a Saturday in late February of 1989 when I finally snapped, cracked up, broke down, flipped out, went around the bend: choose your euphemism. Maxey was away, in North Carolina. I had driven to Nashville to meet my friend Sidney for a movie. I ate lots of malted milk balls and popcorn and drank a big Coke. It's possible that the movie was "The Little Mermaid." It's irrelevant. I can't pin this one on Hollywood.

On the drive home I felt nervous, jumpy, ill at ease. By the time I reached home I was extremely alert, if you know what I mean. It was early evening. I wandered from room to room, unable to light anywhere. I couldn't sit still.

By bedtime I was a wreck. My heart was taking off and I felt like an electric current was running through my body. I settled into bed, wrote in my journal: "I fear attacks from without and within. Finally there is nowhere else left to run. Trapped with a crazy woman."

Sleep was impossible under these conditions. I lay there for hours, listening to my heart race, and pound, and go in and out of sync. At midnight I called Sidney and told her what was going on. She valiantly tried to do relaxation exercises with me over the phone, which left me wide awake, although she drifted off to sleep briefly. So I guess we were partially successful.

I was wired for sound. My body believed it was being pursued by wild dogs, and reacted appropriately. It was only following orders.

Throughout the night sleep evaded me. By six a.m. I could no longer tolerate lying there waiting to die, so I got up and drove the twenty miles to Sidney's house and collapsed on her sofa. I needed the calming presence of another human if for no other reason than the assurance that I would not die alone.

The day remains a blur. Maxey arrived at Sidney's, heavy-laden with worry and guilt. We went home; I set up camp on my own sofa. I was worn slap out. It is terrifying when your body's natural shutoff valves get stuck in the open position. It's a roller coaster ride, sitting stock still, without the fun. That time was, for me, what polite society used to call a "nervous breakdown." I called it "Daniel in the Lion's Den While Actually Undergoing a Crisis of Faith." My monster had grown to such proportions that it blocked out the light. It was a towering giant, threatening to topple and crush me at any second.

The following morning I gamely arose, showered, and while putting on my makeup, started to tremble violently. I went to Maxey in tears. He put his arms around me, but I was beyond consolation. I could not go to work, could not even finish dressing. I was crazy. I had lost the ability to accessorize. I would have to go on disability. I would wear stripes and plaids together and not care. It was the beginning of the end.

Maxey drove me into town to see my doctor. Hmmm, he said. You're in the middle of a panic cycle that has to be broken, he said. He ordered some Xanax for me and arranged for me to be hospitalized overnight.

I went home to get my nightgown. I was nearly giddy with relief (and Xanax). The war was over, and I had lost. I was nuts, and it was going on my permanent record. I would lie in bed and take drugs and have food brought in to me on trays. It was humiliating, and great. So this is what it's like to snap, I thought. I had expected a little more drama: shouts, recriminations, broken crockery, perhaps even stitches. Snapping, in fact, was entirely restful.

# PART TWO:

# RESURGENCE

*"We have met the enemy, and he is us."*

—*Pogo Possum*

# Chapter 4

Joanne is a bright, attractive lady who I met at a group meeting I attended for awhile. She has panic disorder, and has dedicated all her resources to searching for the Answer with-a-capital-A. She is doing exactly what I used to do, what any of us would do to stop the fear: casting about, buying relaxation tapes, attending lectures, reading through the literature, looking for the cures.

All these things can be helpful. But the fact is that the panic disease takes a long time to construct, and it is made of many different pieces, like a crazy quilt. Each piece, taken singly, is not enough to cause the condition. One event, one cup of coffee, one death in the family, one anything can't bring it about. But when several factors converge — put them all together they spell PANIC...

Here is one reason it is such a difficult disease to treat: you attack one symptom and another magically appears. We go from one specialist to another, throwing medicines at different systems, believing it *must* be a physical problem, it must be our inner ears or our hearts or our colons, because if it is not we must be mentally ill. And being crazy is number two on our top ten fear list, second only to death. What a choice: am I mad, or only terminally ill?

What I had to learn, and hope Joanne has learned, is the truth is that there is no truth. No easy way out. No answer in the back of the book. You must be open to many things, take parts and pieces and weave them together into something that works for you. This a long process, but in the end you will have a coat of many colors which will protect you, because it is made with love, and by your own hands.

So the following afternoon I came home from the hospital. Back to the world. I was a little watchful, vigilant, feeling like a soldier returning to the smoking ruins of a battlefield: there might be live ammo lying about. I was still taking the Xanax, .25 mg four times a day. I wanted it to be the solution. I wanted to believe an overnight hospital stay healed me.

I stayed home from work the rest of the week. I still carried some residual fear that I would again be seized with panic, that my heart would begin to race out of control, that the fear would overwhelm me. From this safe distance it is so easy to see how I was brought to my knees on that Saturday night: I was alone, I had had too much caffeine, my hormones were raging out of control, the patients at work kept on dying. And I had panic disorder. I didn't know any of those things at the time, couldn't make the connection. Astounding. Predictable.

As the week wore on I began to notice something strange, unlike all my previous symptoms. About an hour before the scheduled dose of Xanax, I began feeling uncomfortable and agitated. This was not like anxiety. I wanted to curl up in a corner and be left alone. Any stimulation, especially conversation, was difficult. Within minutes of taking the Xanax the feeling disappeared completely.

But it returned repeatedly, right on schedule. Sometimes I had to pace, sometimes I sat and trembled, sometimes I felt like I would jump out of my skin. I knew better than to increase the Xanax on my own, so I started breaking the pills in half and taking them every two hours instead of four. It helped only a little. I believe now I was experiencing withdrawal symptoms between doses because my dosage was too low: remember, .25 mg four times a day. One milligram daily.

It was in this sorry state that I returned to work at hospice. I went through a Jekyll-to-Hyde routine several times a day. You can imagine how useful I was to the dying and their grieving families. I was flat out of ideas about what to do next. I'd used up all my options:

I'd cracked up, been hospitalized, and taken medication — and still was vacillating between fear and worse fear. I was at the edge of the end.

And then the door swung open. At work I was discussing a case I shared with Nita, one of the hospice nurses. And Nita said (out of the blue) Did you know his daughter has panic attacks? I was stunned, and then Nita said *she* had panic attacks. I caved. I told her everything. And Nita told me of a wonderful doctor she had found, and would I like his number? I felt like I'd been wandering in the desert and just spotted a Seven-Eleven. I had an option. I had been given one more chance.

On one of the worst mornings of my life I dialed his office, hands trembling. My life was at stake here. I got his receptionist. He's not taking any new patients, she said. Period. What could I say? My last desperate cry for help was about to end with a dial tone. I began to weep audibly, shamelessly. She said she'd get back to me.

In the end they took me in, and by phone, same day, he doubled my Xanax to two milligrams daily. I wanted this man canonized, and I'd never even seen his face.

About two weeks later I was dressing very carefully, preparing for my first appointment at the Vanderbilt Mood Disorders Clinic. What do you wear to a meeting with your own dark side? Once there, a directory on the wall caught my eye. It listed two of the psychiatrists:

Drs. Loosen and Hammer. I thought this was hilarious. But when I related it to a friend, I got a bewildered stare. Panic humor.

First I met with the psychologist, a thin, poised, dark-haired woman of about thirty. No-nonsense. Her specialty was cognitive therapy, or how to overwhelm the panic monster with reasoning. This truly can be useful if, while under siege, you can think clearly enough to use it. I couldn't, usually, so she gave me some alternatives I'll describe in a moment.

Denise, that's her real name, Denise, talked some about the relationship between our thoughts and the panic attack. You know the drill: the instant the fear begins, we supply a soundtrack and cast of supporting actors. *In the elevator*: Oh no! What if the elevator gets stuck? What if I faint in front of all these people? *In the car*: Oh no! I can't breathe! The car is generating some sort of deadly fumes! What if I lose control and hit that old lady and her Chihuahua? *In the meeting:* Two more people and then it's my turn to introduce myself. Oh no! My heart is beating too fast! Look, my nail beds are turning blue! I think my arm is going numb! Is this a stroke?

You get the picture. You have these, and many more scenarios, maybe even worse. The other day I was talking with a friend and confided that once I was afraid I had swallowed some broken glass and would have internal injuries. (In fact, I *had* found glass pieces in the salad I was eating and got a free lunch.) She said, "Oh, I *hate* that one!" We both laughed.

Logic does have some power if administered properly. A bludgeon, i.e. "Don't be ridiculous," is ineffective. It only serves to make us embarrassed as well as scared. A gentle nudge, such as "I believe you could tell if you had swallowed glass," or even "Some people eat glass for a living" is more useful.

With practice you can find the right sentences, even teach them to your loved ones who can coach you through. The words can become a sort of mantra, a kind of protection to help you.

Anyway, after Denise and I had talked a while about the value of being reasonable, I was sent along to my new doctor, name of Rick Shelton. I can't ever remember his title. I'll have to look it up. He could have been the Chief of Psychiatry or Medical Director of something. He could have been the Grand Poobah of the Knights of the Living Dead for all I cared, if he knew a way out of this thing.

So there was Rick: mid-thirties, baby-faced, with the lithe limbs of a runner, unpretentious haircut; confident without being cocky, sympathetic without being maudlin. Someone you could trust.

It was simple: I gave him the standard history, he told me I had panic disorder. The relief I felt was enormous. Someone may have said this to me sometime before, but I heard it for the first time this day. Just having a name for the monster diminished it a little. And having Rick felt a little like having a bodyguard. He was fearless.

Together — and I can't emphasize the importance of the concept enough — we came up with a plan of attack. Rick has had great success with the use of cognitive therapy coupled with medication. Some people only need the counseling component of the treatment, but I was not one of them. After eleven years of constant barrage, my nervous system was shot. It needed medication like a broken arm needs a cast. The theory goes like this: the medication relieves your symptoms so you have the energy and clarity to learn to deal with the disorder without distraction.

So our plan was for me to see Denise every couple of weeks, and continue the Xanax. I was still on 2 mg. daily. After I settled down a little more we would begin the switch over to Klonipin, a kind of second cousin to Xanax. Klonipin is an anti-anxiety medication with a more gradual release schedule than Xanax, which can have a kind of roller coaster effect. It tends to flame and then die relatively quickly, and you often become physically dependent on it. I agreed to give the Klonipin a shot.

---

But first, Maxey and I took a few days off to go to the beach in search of respite from the wreckage of my life. We needed privacy to begin to mend some of the rips and tears that had occurred during my hand-to-hand combat with this illness. We stayed four days. On our last evening I went to the beach alone, and drew peace signs in the sand with my toes. As I was leaving, a guy passed me, stopped, and turned. "Taking the leaving walk, eh?" he said. I said "You can spot 'em, can't you?" Then he said, "You want to talk?" I hesitated. "Talk to me!" he said. And just for that moment I believed I lived in a world where you could tell a stranger you had this symbiotic twin, this panic monster, attached to your chest, an imaginary playmate from a nightmare, and that the stranger would not start backing away slowly, nodding, eyes betraying the fear inside. I'm fine, I said. Fine. And walked on.

The hell I was. The following day I had a panic attack while driving back home. Maxey was sleeping. I was turning into the parking lot of a restaurant for lunch when it struck. Suddenly, as always, I felt that familiar tingling in my solar plexus, felt it radiating to my limbs, felt the fear spreading like a flash fire. My heart began racing and I felt faint. Maxey, poor guy, had had more pleasant wake-up calls. He sighed deeply, hurt that he could not make it stop, tired of having to deal with it. I added guilt to the emotions zooming through me like I was the Indy 500. Always room for one more.

I sat at the table in the restaurant unable to eat, ashamed, while Maxey ate his lunch in silence. When we left I took a sandwich with me, knowing that when the fear finally subsided I would be hungry again.

I started on the Klonipin near the end of March. At first the adjustment was difficult: with Xanax you know you've taken the medicine and help is on the way. Not so with Klonipin. You take it and hope and pray it will kick in when you need it most.

Initially I allowed myself a little optimism. I wrote in my journal: "I find I'm changing in little ways — I've stopped taking my temperature, and for a crazy while it was ten or fifteen times a day, no kidding. I'm not so afraid of my body, so my body is not so afraid of me. I may — I just may — be able to find a new life, finally, one that is completely my own."

I took the Klonipin all through April before I realized I was crying very often. I was exhausted. I had dreams of blood. We finally figured out that the Klonipin was making me depressed, and Rick stopped it and put me back on the Xanax. Listen: with this disorder, finding the right medication and dosage can be very difficult and tedious. It takes a long time — weeks, usually — to see how your body will adjust, and even then you must be able to separate the fear symptoms from the physical ones. It requires courage, persistence, and patience. Since the alternative involves crawling around on your hands and knees crying, "I'm so dizzy," it becomes a relatively easy choice.

Initially my Xanax dose was a little low, so it was a bit of a struggle until we raised it to three mg. daily. That amount seemed to hold the monster in check and still allow me to work and go out in public with a minimum of discomfort. I did not feel great. Remember, there is no magic cure. Trusting that your medicine will not let you down is a leap of faith only you can make. And Rick and I had a fallback plan: soon I would start on the antidepressant.

Rick had been very forthright with me about the effects antidepressants have on panickers. Generally the breaking-in period is rough, because the drug actually produces and intensifies panic symptoms for several days, overstimulating receptors until they shut down, which then blocks the panic message when it tries to get through. In effect, the monster knocks but nobody answers. This is why antidepressants work. But let me tell you, the idea of actually *causing* panic symptoms to appear for several days was daunting. Really it was beyond daunting, and went all the way to terrifying. Imagine: your worst fears, and you bring them on intentionally. What will they think of next?

A week before I started the new medication, my two sisters and I converged for a first-time-ever vacation together. There is a place in the mountains of North Carolina called the Pisgah View Ranch. It's a wonderful place, pretty isolated, pretty old, where you stay in cabins with names and screened-in porches and knotty pine paneling and eat fabulous meals, boarding-home style. It's miles from nowhere.

Doris and I met in Knoxville and drove over to the ranch

together. Louise was coming from South Carolina. When she arrived three hours late, she told us her car had broken down on the interstate, and it had taken all her vacation money to fix it. We hoped it was not an omen.

We three sisters are close, and fiercely loyal, and overly sensitive. Louise lit a cigarette upon awakening each morning, and this really got next to Doris. (Louise has long since quit smoking.) Doris read road signs aloud until I thought we actually might strike her. (She dropped the habit later.) And I had a panic attack in the middle of nowhere, complete with rocking and moaning. After the initial show of concern, my sisters trotted off to dinner, where, I presume, they ate heartily. They brought me crackers, and I was grateful.

But here's the thing: we each showed our house specialty, did what we were best, and worst, at. It was as though we distilled our personalities and we were more like we are than we ever had been: on stage, so every nuance, every gesture was exaggerated. Each of us would gladly hand over a kidney if the situation called for it. Unfortunately, the situation only called for us to be civil for seventy-two hours.

Still, we laughed an awful lot. We made much over Louise's wonderful sketches. We wore each other's clothes and took pictures of everything.

And declared, at the end, that we would do it all over again. We have to. Our genes overlap. Hey, Doc, we were born this way.

# *Chapter 5*

Finally I could put it off no longer. I had to start taking the antidepressant. Let me throw in this piece of information: it has been my experience that all the people I know with panic disorder are also afraid, nay, terrified, of medicine. We're afraid of adverse reactions, of deadly accidental combinations, of overdoses, of poisoned Tylenol. We are hard put to take simple things like antibiotics. Most of us are familiar with the term "anaphylactic shock." We usually manage to have access to PDRs (Physicians Desk Reference), the drug encyclopedia. The sections on adverse reactions have a special place in our hearts. The law of panic is: you read it, you've got it.

Rick tried his best to prepare me for the side effects of the new medication. You walk a fine line when you give information like this to panic people. Some information comforts and dispels fears. Too much just gives us ideas. And in the end you just do it, and hope for the best.

I took my first 25 mg. capsule of Pamelor on a Saturday night. I remember swallowing it. I sat at the dining room table, afraid to move, feeling like Alice in Wonderland, ready to shrink or swell. Nothing happened. And nothing continued to happen until the third or fourth day, when my heart began racing. I took my pulse constantly, which of course made it race even faster, and though I felt like I was on a train out of control, I probably never broke a hundred. A couple of times I had episodes of dizziness and feared I would faint, but I didn't. When I wasn't taking my pulse I was driving around trying to visit hospice patients, and it seemed I called Rick from every pay phone in West Nashville. He was infinitely patient, constantly reassuring, and said things like Great! It's working! As long as I knew that, I could stand the racing pulse, the dry, clicking mouth, the tremors. I believed him when he said these symptoms would pass, and my faith was well-placed.

I stayed on the 25 mg. dosage of Pamelor for a week before we bumped it up to 50 mg. Rick said it took about five days for the level of the drug to build up in your system. One drawback is that it takes three to six weeks to find out if it's working properly. Six weeks is a long time to be edgy. Ask my husband. But we knew it was necessary.

Pamelor initially overstimulates and sedates you by turns. For a few days I'd come home from work and sleep for a couple of hours. It passes in time. After several weeks you lose some of the side effects. The racing heart, the nervousness, the sleepiness passes. The dry mouth, a symptom I never experienced with the panic attacks, remains. I had to drink lots of water and eat carefully or my insides would shut down faster than a Savings and Loan. You find ways to adjust. I'll say more about diet later.

There is another symptom I should mention because it can really scare you as well as your bedmate. One night I woke up about 12:30 a.m. with a terrible ache in my chest. It felt like someone was squeezing my heart. Imagine waking abruptly in the dead of night with severe chest pain. What do we call these, class? *Warning* signals, maybe?

The first time it happened I lay there waiting to die. After awhile I got tired of waiting and got up and walked around some. It was a severe pain, really intense about two seconds after I swallowed. I realized I was feeling my esophagus clench in a spasm just beneath my breastbone. I called Sidney, who has the ability to be reasonable just moments after she has been awakened from a deep sleep. She confirmed the spasm diagnosis and recommended hot tea. I tried it, but it was still so painful when I swallowed the tea that I abandoned the treatment plan. Finally I figured out that if I propped up in the bed with pillows, almost sitting upright, I could go to sleep.

The pain came back a few times, but usually when I had not drunk enough liquid when taking the Pamelor. Rick confirmed this phenomenon, even said someone was studying it. Another lesson for me. At least I have no shortage of *those*.

Even if you are using medication and having some side effects, it's still more than an even trade. When it finally begins to work, you will be stunned by the amount of energy you have to do other things, like not be scared. This disease takes all your will, and imagination, and courage, just to get through the day. You don't realize how much it has stolen from you until it begins to return. You will dance and sing when you begin to rediscover what you had lost. Once Rick asked me how my life would be different if I didn't have this disease. And I said, It's not so much that I would *do* anything differently — it's just that I would live more deeply. I don't miss parasailing or bungee jumping or those "wilderness challenge" weekends where they don't let you wear makeup. I just want to be able to take a shower in peace. I want to sit down at a family dinner without fear of fear overtaking me. I want to relax.

The marvel of this medicine thing is that when you know it's working, it's as though somebody chained up the panic monster and you can poke sticks at it and go Nyah, Nyah, and although it may lunge, it can't get you. It rises up, and then it stops. The medicine defines the response, making it physically impossible for the panic to rise beyond a certain level. Once you learn to trust this response, you can go do those things you didn't have the heart or the courage for. You will live your life more deeply, and marvel at what most people take for granted.

Now that I've said all these great things about medication, I need to point out that many people can get along just fine without it. Sometimes cognitive therapy, learning to re-think your responses, is enough. And there are lots of tricks you can use, like the record-keeping I'll mention later. I don't think they know why some people need medication and others don't. I thought perhaps it depended upon the length of time you had had panic disorder, figuring that the longer the duration, the more damaged your nervous system is. But Rick says this is not so; duration alone does not determine the treatment most effective for you. And too, I'd been in talk therapy three different times over the past twenty years or so, and while it was helpful in many ways, it never did a thing for the panic. The thing of it is, even if you could pin this disease on some poorly-concealed childhood secret, *the knowledge alone does not make it stop.* The attacks are a physical response, a nervous system careening out of control, and even though your mind is jumping to conclusions, your body started it. And I'll probably say this over and over, because you need to hear it repeatedly: it's not your fault. It's not anyone's fault.

To the casual observer it may appear that panic sufferers do it for the attention. What they fail to understand is that while under attack, we would rather die than admit in public that we are fixing to die, which is why we speedwalk out of restaurants still chewing, terrified that someone will see us being terrified. Humiliation is but one byproduct of this capricious disorder.

And the reason we confess our fears over and over to those trusted few, who even if they don't completely understand, don't run away screaming or slip off quietly to dial 911, is because we need somebody to say these words to us: "You're okay, you're just having a panic attack. You're not having a stroke (heart attack, intestinal bleeding, hysterical blindness, you fill in your personal preference.)" We can't trust our own judgment. We need a second opinion. It's a tricky thing: if I'm having an attack and I call Rick, all he has to say is You're having an attack and this is normal and you'll be fine in a few minutes. And I will be. When I try to tell myself these things, the response is Who do you think you are? And often, You think that one was bad, try *this* one.

I learned a valuable lesson one night when I went to the walking track alone, hoping the exercise would help discharge some of the nervous energy I was feeling. The track was nearly deserted. Halfway through the second lap, when I was the greatest possible distance from my car, the monster started his panic rap, his patter:

What if I faint here, on the track? What if I can't make it back to the car? What if — and luckily, at that moment, a hard-shelled bug flew into my eye and lodged there, displacing fear with extreme pain. In that moment I recognized yet another treatment modality for this disease: if somebody would whack me in the head with a two-by-four every fifteen minutes, I'm confident all panic symptoms would vanish.

---

There are certain inescapable evenings, like tonight, when I have been anxious all day, off-center, and edgy; when I am so defeated by this disorder that it feels like I am flat on my back and the monster is crouching on my chest. It is beyond discouraging. I see my life stretch before me and believe it will always be a choice between medication and fear. I think I will never be free. My thoughts are dark and heavy; I am weary and hopeless and finally, angry. I welcome the anger, feed it, because I know it is a path leading back into the world. It will mobilize me eventually, taunt me into getting up, bully me into stepping into the shower, goad me to the grocery store.

Sometimes these spells will break under their own weight, sometimes not. What we fail to remember is that people without this disorder also will have whole days of feeling edgy and nervous, a little peckish. For them, it passes without a second thought. They don't imagine brain tumors or MS or insanity. We are so attuned to monitoring our bodily goings-on that it becomes a full-time job, because changes happen constantly. It's called homeostasis. Our hearts speed up, slow down, kick in an extra beat. We heat up, cool down; blood pressure varies from moment to moment. All this means nothing. Our bodies are designed to compensate constantly for changing conditions, always striving for self-preservation. I've seen what people have to go through to die, and sometimes it is unbelievable. I've seen people live for weeks on two sips of coffee each day. And I drop two pounds and think I have colon cancer. When logic is applied, we come up a little short. I mean in 1978 I honestly wondered if I would live to see Christmas, and by now you'd think I'd have figured out that my odds are pretty good. But that's logic. Problem is you feel the fear so quickly when it comes over you that it's difficult to be reasonable. Your body is so caught up in the fight-or-flight preparations that it rolls over your puny logic like a Mack Truck over a possum. Yes, your intellect is reduced to road kill.

I'll tell you an exercise that Denise gave me during my cognitive therapy session which actually helps. But first —

My husband showed me a cartoon of a spotted leopard, frantic, pacing, musing to himself: "Spotted fever; I just *know* I've got Spotted fever."

Panic humor: don't leave home without it.

Here is a useful tool that can help you think rationally instead of going off like a loose cannon every five seconds at the first hint of an attack. Get a little notebook and carry it with you all the time. Take it out as soon as you feel your symptoms start up, or as soon as you are able, and follow this outline:

| | |
|---|---|
| DATE: | FEELINGS: |
| TIME: | THOUGHTS: |
| LOCATION: | ALTERNATIVES: |
| SITUATION: | PROBABLE CAUSES: |

Documentation does a couple of things for you. One, it gives you something to do, which helps distract you from your panic attack. Two, it makes you analyze the attack so it loses some of its power over you. The power that fuels the panic comes from your own fear. Reduce your fear and you can at least partially, if not completely, derail the attack.

---

I swear these work. Here's one I did:

DATE: 4-21-89        TIME: 11:30 a.m.
LOCATION: Hospice office
SITUATION: I was charting in a patients' record, stood up quickly to talk to another social worker about a case. Felt dizzy and started to panic.
FEELINGS: Dizziness, fear, detached from reality.
THOUGHTS: This should not be happening since I'm on

medication. I have to give a talk this afternoon. What if it happens there? What if it gets worse?

ALTERNATIVES: Sit quietly for a few minutes. Relax your shoulders. Stop working. Walk around outside.

PROBABLE CAUSES: I stood up too quickly. Pamelor can cause temporary blood pressure drops under these conditions. I'm nervous about giving the talk this afternoon. I'm writing chart notes about dying people.

Okay. This one is more revealing and therefore more embarrassing, but it's for a good cause.

DATE: 4-25-89
TIME: 5:00 p.m.
LOCATION: Driving home from work.
SITUATION: My legs became extremely weak, then my arms felt so heavy I could barely hold the steering wheel.
FEELINGS: Panic; extreme fatigue; wanting to cry.
THOUGHTS: What if this is Guillian-Barré Syndrome and I become paralyzed? I can't do anything — pretty soon I won't even be able to walk. I'm so *exhausted*. There's no reason for this to happen. (See the recurring theme?) Maybe I have a tumor on my spine like the girl I visited this afternoon.
ALTERNATIVES: Lie down and rest for a few minutes. Be distracted by other things. Cry. Make sure you've had enough to eat.
PROBABLE CAUSE: I walked a lot today and work was more stressful than I thought. I was okay this afternoon so I probably didn't develop a disease in the last hour.

You can use this outline to talk yourself down when an attack comes on. The alternatives are especially helpful because you can see that you still have some choices, and choice implies control. The fear loses some of its power when you shine a light on it.

I used this exercise many times when I started out with Rick and Denise. I needed it less and less as time went on. I began doing it in my head instead of writing it out. It helps me to remember I have this tool, and how effective it is. I'll put the outline at the end of the book so you can copy it or tear it out to carry with you.

# Chapter 6

What I want to discuss next is the importance of finding the right person to work with you. Just arriving at the correct diagnosis can be difficult enough, as we all know. It comes through trial and error, checking out physical symptoms, and good history-taking to sort through the facts and fallacies that make up your life. Once diagnosed, you will need someone to help you. It can be a psychiatrist, psychologist, social worker, counselor, whatever. But whomever you choose, this person must have special knowledge of panic disorder; must have treated many people before you; must possess infinite patience and openmindedness; and must inspire trust. I can't stress enough how invaluable these characteristics are. This is not the time to cut corners.

I have a friend whose symptoms were so severe that she could not drive to her job. She was taking her temperature dozens of times each day. Sometimes she hyperventilated to the point of fainting. It took quite a while for me to convince her that she needed someone who understood her condition. Until that time she had been using the local emergency room and her family doctor almost weekly.

She found a psychiatrist approved by her insurance company who told her he specialized in the treatment of panic disorder. He told her to bring $140.00 to her first appointment.

After their first meeting she reported that he took some basic history, but was not interested in her current marital difficulties, nor her sister's recent suicide attempt. The fact that three generations of her family are riddled with alcoholism, drug abuse, depression, panic and divorces was not explored. When she asked him a question, he cut her off: I'll ask the questions here, he said. And in the end he prescribed Tofranil, up to four a day. And the .5 mg Xanax she already had? Up to four a day if you want to, he said.

Like most of us, this young woman was terrified of any kind of medication, and tended to undermedicate herself if she took anything. She gamely tried the Tofranil. But on the second night she awoke to find her arms and legs numb, shook her husband awake, and make him fill the tub with steaming water. The heat helped return the feeling to her limbs, but did little to dispel her fright.

The following day was a Saturday. She contacted the doctor

through his answering service, and he changed her dosage by phone. Things did not improve. On Monday, she tried repeatedly to reach him, and finally had to call him through his service again Monday evening. When he returned her call he was clearly peeved and said she had to stop calling him at home. "Panic attacks won't kill you," he said.

She felt humiliated, furious, and disillusioned with doctors. I was afraid she'd never go back to anyone. Luckily, her symptoms were so disruptive she finally agreed to go to the clinic at Vanderbilt where Rick's practice is. She got an appointment within ten days.

Her new doc is calm, and interested in what she has to say, and reassuring. He is helping her adjust to her medication. After just two weeks I can already see some changes in her, although at this point she is still more likely to point out the problems that remain. That's normal. I asked her to keep a journal so she could look back periodically and see the differences in her life. It's a remarkable process, viewed from the safety of a little distance.

Here is my point: find someone who knows what he/she is doing. If there is a medical school or teaching hospital nearby, you're in luck. Call them and find out who's specializing in panic disorder. There may be a Psychological Association or a branch office of the National Association of Social Workers. Look in the Yellow Pages. Call a couple of (or several) therapists and ask who does treatment in this area. If you use someone who cannot prescribe medication, make sure they have access to someone who can, if you need it. In Nashville we have a wonderful association called Agoraphobics in Action, which puts out an invaluable newsletter and has quarterly meetings with knowledgeable speakers. They also maintain a crisis call line for information. Your area may have something comparable. Use it.

If you're like me, you've tried to get by using your family doctor or gynecologist. For years I had caring, learned doctors treating my various complaints. They kept me afloat, but in the end I needed a specialist. This is not a disease you can throw a couple of Xanax at and have it go away. It demands major, permanent life changes. It is as exacting as diabetes, or high blood pressure, or any chronic disorder. My point is that the course is not easy. You must be diligent. There is no fast fix. It's a slow process, because just as the panic disorder invades every part of your life, so must the treatment. As you come to recognize one symptom, it loses its power to make you afraid, and so a new symptom takes its place. It's enough to try your patience and heaven knows the patience of those who have to live with you has been worn threadbare in places. With or without medication the process is tough. Sometimes I think panic attacks are the price we pay for being too sensitive, both physically and emotionally, to our world. When I was a child in school, I cried if the child next to me cried. The pain of another was enough to move me to tears. It still can, but unfortunately,

I have learned better how not to cry.

———————

Well, let's change the subject. It's August, 1989. I've just been offered a position at the hospital in the little town where we live. I'm ready to let go of hospice work, ready to work where I live for a change. It's a part-time job, and the hospital has only twenty-nine beds and four doctors. I'm scared to death because of my last experience working in a hospital. This will have to be different, I think, I pray. I believe I can do this. I want it to be a place where I can heal some of my damaged nervous system. Maybe I'm hoping for too much.

The administrator says: What do you say? I say: Okay. I'll take it.

By late fall of that year my job at the hospital was working nicely and life was beginning to seem pretty good. My panic was under control for the most part. I was seeing Rick only once a month, often just for fifteen or twenty minute visits, discussing the medication, monitoring my progress. But there was a fly on the horizon, a cloud in the ointment, a hitch in the gitalong: in January my husband, my safe person, my voice of reason, was going away to Washington, D.C., for three months. Ninety days. And nights.

There is an excellent movie called "The Bear" in which an orphaned cub is befriended by a huge adult bear. The cub observes the bear, mimics him, learns how to defend himself. In the end the cub is being pursued by a cougar. Finally, with no exits left, the cub turns, rears up on his hind legs, and faces the cougar. The cat beats a retreat. And then the camera pans back to reveal the huge grizzly standing behind the cub. Of course it is he who has frightened away the cougar.

This was my fear: that I believed I could hold the panic monster at bay, but the reality was that it was my husband who was protecting me. And that without him the monster would show me no mercy.

*"Word I was in the house alone*
*Somehow must have gotten abroad,*
*Word I was in my life alone,*
*Word I had no one left but God."*
— Robert Frost

So in early January of 1990 I put Maxey on a plane to D.C. The first night he was gone I dreamed I stuffed a baby's sleeper pajamas with New Age pamphlets until the arms and legs stuck straight out. Then I handed it to some man to carry because it was "too heavy" for me. I can always count on my dreams for some dime store revelations.

The first several nights alone I awoke with my heart racing, but each time I managed to get back to sleep. My fear was that I would die alone in the night and no one would find me for days. (It's always the meter reader or the garbage guy who reports a "foul odor" emanating from the house. I don't wish my last act on this earth to be offending my neighbors.)

Sidney, my good friend, has a dread that she will die and that her dog, driven by starvation, will begin to snack on her. She doesn't begrudge the dog his meal, but rather hates to think of the trauma to whomever happens upon the scene.

It was clear to me that I was going to need some help through these months alone. I had met Lesley through my work with hospice. She had panic disorder also, and through Agoraphobics in Action she had gotten the names of several people who were interested in starting a kind of leaderless support group. We began meeting once a week at Lesley's home. I called us affectionately, publicly and privately, the Crazy Ladies Group. We numbered about five, give or take. Our youngest was Stacey, at seventeen. Her mother drove her to the meetings and sat out in the car until we finished. Remember, this was in January. She bought Stacey an expensive puppy, which she brought to a meeting: We will try anything to make the fear go away. So will our loved ones.

Lesley was afraid to drive alone. If one of her children were with her, she was fine. For weeks her father followed her to work in his car, and met her after work to follow her home. The times she had to drive alone, she constantly scanned her surroundings for people who might help her if she had an attack.

Anita was impeccably dressed, obviously wealthy, and desperate. The attacks were destroying her life. And she had a crisis coming up: her daughter lived in Europe, and she was planning a trip to visit her. But this involved flying, and across the Atlantic. Anita was in a constant state of controlled terror.

We even had a man come to a couple of meetings. He's the only man I've met who admits to having panic disorder. His terror — and his willingness to share this with a bunch of women went beyond courageous — was that he would be somewhere, on a boat, on a tour, and would suddenly have need of a restroom, and there would be no restroom. This was his worst fear, but they're all basically the same one. It just dresses up in different outfits. Losing control. It takes many forms, as many as the imagination can encompass. Strip the panic monster of his disguises, his very flesh; leave only the skeleton. Sunk deep into those bones, the glue that holds them together, the marrow, there it is: the fear of losing control.

A few times we invited guests to the group. I took Sidney once, a kind of show and tell, so she could talk to us about stress management. As I recall, she couldn't get a word in edgewise. People who panic, when they find each other, can't stop talking. Finally: someone who speaks the language, knows the customs. Someone who can laugh out loud at your latest, most outrageous symptom and then top it.

These women were kind, bright, pretty, and funny. Nobody

held back. With them I no longer felt alone, and most remarkable of all, I felt at ease. Nobody had an attack at these meetings. We circled our wagons and kept the bonfire blazing.

The group did so much to keep me going those months without Maxey. We exchanged survival tips like recipes at a church social. We said our most irrational fears out loud, and laughed at the outrageous behaviors we resorted to in order to live.

The Crazy Ladies Group dwindled and died after a couple of months, but it was a natural, painless death. Someday we may have a reunion.


If I were relying on memory alone, I would recall that I got through those months with few problems. But that's not what I read in my journal. I read that I woke often in the night with my heart racing. That several nights I got up and tried to sleep on the couch because my stomach was upset. That every night I awoke at 1:30, 3:15, and 5:30, afraid. And that I stayed up later and later, hoping it would help me sleep through the night. During the days, several times I felt the wave of panic rise within me, and each time I sat still, holding my breath, praying the monster wouldn't spot me. And after a few moments, the wave would subside.

My medicine was working. Here is the way I envisioned it: I saw my brain as a series of passageways leading to the center where fear resides. These passages were worn slick as a waterslide from such frequent use. The medicine set up blockages so that new passageways had to be developed, ones that bypassed the fear center. And as soon as these new roadways were firmly established, I wouldn't need the medicine any more. It's not scientific. It's not anatomically correct. It's a fantasy about what goes on inside my head, and it helped me believe my life could change. Why is it so easy to believe I will drop dead, and so difficult to believe that I will live to see another spring?

Okay. Here's a fairly recent example of how the attacks affect me now. One morning I woke up at 5:25 a.m. and I felt a headache start. It began between my eyes and spread to my temples and cheekbones. Everything north of my nose felt like an ill-fitting Halloween mask. The fear started; the familiar tingling began, and with it came the thoughts: maybe a blood vessel in my head has ruptured. And then I imagined overlighted emergency rooms, spinal taps, paralysis. I knew if I took an aspirin it would thin my blood and make the internal bleeding even worse.

This is the dark side of an imagination combined with a little bit of knowledge. And when the monster jolts me out of a sound sleep, he has a definite edge. I'm disoriented; my defenses are down. I am Pearl Harbor on a Sunday morning.

Anyway, I got up and looked in the bathroom mirror to see if my pupils were equal in size. I took my temperature, just for something to do. It was normal. So I went back to bed and curled up next to Maxey like Calvin to Hobbes.

The headache remained until I got to work, where I finally took an aspirin and became involved in the problems of the patients. It was a mild attack, as they go.

Then I made myself reason it out, examining it as though it had happened to somebody else. You have to separate to see clearly. And this is what I saw:

— One of my sister's friends had a malignant brain tumor and was dying. Two days earlier I had put together a packet for her on disability benefits, a bibliography of books on grief, and a review of a book called *Living with Dying*.

— At work I was seeing a fifty-year-old woman who was dying of lymphoma. Another had died the previous week. And I was unsuccessful in finding a rehabilitation center for a forty-year-old woman who had had a stroke. Forty.

So I looked at all these factors and thought, Oh yeah, of course you'd think you were having a cerebral bleed. These are all terrifying and disruptive thoughts, and they manifest as a ruptured blood vessel. It's like that automatic bread-making machine: you dump in all the ingredients, and what comes out is completely different. Only instead of a loaf of the bread I get some life-threatening condition.

But here's my point (and not a moment too soon, you say).

Four years ago I would've experienced that episode quite differently. My fear would have escalated, continued throughout the day, produced other fears until I exhausted my own imagination. Nowadays, mostly, I feel the fear but can also stand back and take a look at what's going on, what's really bothering me. Armed with reason, I can more easily let the fear pass. I expect I may always have the symptoms. Unfortunately, understanding the reasons still doesn't prevent the attacks, but it can help reduce them to a manageable level. With practice you can shrink the monster by a good 50 percent.

# Chapter 7

When I was in the fifth grade, I had a teacher named Miss Davidson. She was somewhere between forty and sixty and wore her waist-length hair tightly braided into a bun at the nape of her neck. Anyway, the year was 1958 and World War II hadn't been over all that long even by a child's standard. She intended to read us a poem about the war, but warned us that once she had read it to a class and children had wept because they had lost relatives in the war. You can guess the rest. She read the poem, I cried, and she leaned over my desk, patted me on the shoulder, and whispered "Let's just be glad it's over."

Well, I felt like a thief. I had lost no loved ones in the war. I wasn't even *born* yet. But the mere suggestion that I might cry was sufficient to bring it on. If someone remarked that I looked a little feverish, I got one. If I read about a side effect or an adverse reaction,

I get it. I've found several women with panic disorder who have this same quality. The second someone (almost anyone, including total strangers) suggests the slightest abnormality. The fear hits, the questions begin. Am I really sick? Is there something wrong with my (heart, lungs, blood, lymph glands, Islet of Langerhans, etc.)? And we escalate to the self-performed mini-physical. (I have a thermometer in my desk drawer at work, don't you?) We count our heartbeats. We peer at the whites of our eyes for any sign of jaundice. We feel the glands in our necks. You know the drill; you've done it. Maxey says I should have a card to hand out that reads "Please do not make any negative comments about my appearance." He's right. One of the toughest things to do is learn to trust your own judgment in these matters. I've had to learn how to distinguish between fear and illness: what is nausea and what is fright? They feel the same, at least initially. Which is fever and which is the hot flash of fear? And this from my sister Louise, many years ago, as a child: sometimes she didn't know whether she was angry or just hot, because they felt the same.

Suggestibility: I can see everyone's side of the argument, which is very useful in my work, but can be a real drawback after hours. Here is my rational self saying don't listen to that salesman in the bad plaid jacket selling symptoms! Just say no to brain tumors! And my suggestible self is already getting out the checkbook.

What we must learn is how to trust ourselves, to believe we know our bodies better than anyone else, and if we were to become truly ill, we would know it. We are so terrified of being sneaked up on; of being attacked from without as well as from within. Walking the perimeter becomes a full-time, permanent job, and when it exhausts us, we think we have mononucleosis. We can stop now, guys. We can give it a rest. We can stop asking Why is my heart beating so fast or my hands so cold or my feet so hot? The answer is irrelevant. We have panic disorder. It contains multitudes.

There is an excellent suggestion from one of the AIA newsletters. Remember the "what if" refrain? It goes like this: What if my heart stops? What if my throat swells shut? What if I faint and my face falls in my plate? What if everybody thinks I'm crazy? The monster feeds on this stuff like it was Purina Monster Chow. Just keeps on getting bigger. The newsletter suggests that you substitute the words "so what" for "what if." It's good advice. So what if my face is flushed? So what if that pesky vessel ruptures? So what if my mitral valve is clicking like a castanet? With practice, you can pull it off, and the cavalier attitude throws the panic monster into a dither. Take this trick as one more weapon for your arsenal. I'll try to remember to write it down at the end of the book so you can tear the page out and carry it around with you.

The combination of Pamelor and Xanax had worked well for me. For the most part I was panic free, for the first time for over a decade. I even felt strong enough, and bold enough, to begin the long process of getting off the Xanax. I never liked the feeling that I was dependent upon the drug and wanted to be free of it. So in April 1990, Rick and I set down a schedule: reduce the dose by .25 every two weeks. A half milligram a month. At this rate it would take me six months, but I was ready to start: tanned, rested, and ready.

The song says the first cut is always the deepest. To minimize the effects of withdrawal, we had chosen the month of April. The sun is out and generally there's more hope. I took the first cut from my nighttime dose, hoping I could sleep through any rebound. I was wrong. Eighty percent superstition, but I felt it. My period was due (like a bill). Rick said Wait 'til that comes and goes, and give it another shot. After five days I tried again, with more success. I still could feel the difference, but I didn't have the fear.

There's a tendency for panic symptoms to increase when you're reducing your medicine. Expecting the symptoms can make them better or worse to deal with. It helps knowing there is a physical explanation for our panic. Or, you can take the short cut and make your symptoms appear by searching for them. As Maxey said to me, sometimes you just have to push on through. You gut it out.

Here is what I wrote during that interminable process of disengaging from Xanax:

"This is withdrawal. I thought I could skip it, but what the hell. I remember these feelings. A sensation of being off balance slightly, dizzy at times. An inability to focus. Acutely self-conscious. My voice sounds too loud, too resounding. I am afraid my words make little sense. The sensations I note (again) in my body frighten me. I spend a great deal of time checking out a pain in my side, most likely, a slight strain. I think (honestly!) kidney cancer. Where do these come from? I call Sandra, knowing she will present the reasonable side for me. She does. And it helps. I don't like these recent entries. I wanted the fear to disappear. I don't want to believe that it was simply waiting for me, patiently, all these months, knowing its time would come around again. I've worked too hard, been through too much to have that happen. And now I'm feeling out of control and like I will die soon, just because I claim to have lost some of my fear about it.

What if? What if? I forgot the So What? rule. And if my death is so imminent, why did I just spend $56 on beauty products?"

And a few days later:

"Another cutback, another setback. Now the nighttime dose is down to .25. That's not bad. But I wake often and stay awake for what seems a long time. I refuse to be cowed by this medication. I can stand it. It can make me uncomfortable, but it can't make me afraid. Well, okay, maybe a little. But the panic monster has shrunk considerably."

It did take six months to get off the Xanax. I had some skirmishes, but no full-blown attacks that I recall. One night on vacation at the beach I woke up, heart racing, feverish, but nothing much came of it. I woke Maxey and he held me until I went back to sleep. How simple.

From time to time I had the usual fantasies of having MS or whatever debilitating disease was hot, but there was an important difference: I wasn't afraid. There was, instead of panic, just a mild sense of curiosity. Was this what it was like to be normal? You entertain an outlandish idea for a few moments and then discard it? I felt like I was learning a second language.

What I wanted most was a flat place in my life, a plateau, where I could camp out for a while, have no demands on me. I thought if I could just have that, I could heal myself, repair my damaged nervous system, get everything going in the same direction at the same time. It doesn't happen. People get sick; sometimes they die. In medical social work you hear all kinds of dreadful stories. And you get involved because it's what you do. Their pain sticks to the heel of your shoe and you drag it around after you all day. When you go up against panic disorder, it's on-the-job training. You can't dodge some crisis just because your medication isn't regulated or your hormones are in an uproar. You just have to find your way. And sometimes every trick in the book (professionals call it *technique*, or heaven help us, *coping mechanism*) fails you and there you sit, heart pounding, eyes wild, gasping for breath, while the rest of the world hums a merry tune. And you curse this condition, this unfair state of affairs, and you curse those who have never had this feeling of being on the edge of the end. And then you wait for it to pass. That's all. You don't get a month off to get into shape. You get your life, ready or not.

Sometime during the fall of 1990 I took my last dose of Xanax. No parades, no awards, no congratulatory telegrams; just me, proud of the accomplishment, cautiously optimistic. On November 26, I wrote: "I haven't even come close to panic in a very long time. It's true. I'm not the same person in that way anymore. The monster has moved somewhere else. I believe it will return to look in on me now and then, but it will find the windows boarded up and the door nailed shut. Maybe I flatter myself, but I don't think so. There's nothing shallow about hard work, about believing in a different kind of life."

Who was that woman? And how wrong could she be?

By the end of winter, I was down to 25mg. of the Pamelor, and sometimes I skipped doses. I was eager to be free of medication, wanted to see what it would be like after all this time. I felt like an accident victim, both apprehensive and excited about having the bandages removed. I was having an upsurge in symptoms during this time. I got scared of random aches and pains. I started crying more easily, more often. At night sometimes I awoke to feel my heart pounding in my chest, each beat shaking the whole bed. But I was handling the symptoms okay. I avoided the cycle of terror, serpentined so the monster (remember the one who moved out, and only a page ago) never got a direct hit.

I thought I was ready to go it alone. When I had been off the Pamelor completely for a month, Rick thought so too. We had our last appointment on April 29, 1991. As he gave me a backup prescription for Valium, just in case, I said to his receptionist: "Guess what? I'm no longer a work in progress."

On Mother's Day I called Rick on the phone from a restaurant in tears. I was in total despair. I wasn't having actual panic attacks, but I had a bad case of anticipatory anxiety, fear of fear. I was afraid of having a car accident. I had dreams of blood and death. I was disoriented and couldn't concentrate. The monster was back, and so soon! It was staggering.

In retrospect, we should have known that May was not the best month to call it quits. May is the month of my mother's cancer diagnosis. It's the month of our nephews' deaths, and a miscarriage for me. Mother's Day is tossed in there. April is not the cruellest month, as the poem states. I felt like I was choking.

I struggled through spring, refusing to go back into treatment, using the Valium as a stopgap measure, a last resort. It wasn't much help. What to do? I kept hoping it would just go away. I thought maybe it was just my body chemistry rebounding, and if I waited it out, it would stabilize. Like when you're a kid swinging high on your swing set, and you let the cat die. I was waiting for the cat to die.

# Chapter 8

It's a Tuesday morning. I step into the shower, wet my hair. Immediately, I smell a heavy, flowery scent and I begin to feel faint. I get out of the shower pronto, wrap a towel around me, make my way to the bedroom. Waves of dizziness and terror wash over me and my whole body is trembling. I think what I always think: This can't be just a panic attack. Something is *wrong* with me. I wait for the next wave to hit, and I believe I will die here, in this room, alone, with wet hair. I take a Valium, a half at a time. Then I begin to cry, deafening, shaking sobs, and I rock back and forth, asking God for strength and courage. As soon as I begin to calm down, the panic rises again. I search for reasons, answers, anything to explain away this feeling. I need a truth to cling to. Because this means I could prevent it from happening again. An hour ago I was full of plans for the day ahead, anxious to get on with it. Now I honestly wonder if I will live through this onslaught.

A little later I approach the shower, the *other* shower. I turn on the water, turn it off and walk away. But I know this is something I must do. I step into the shower, regulate the water temperature. "I can do this," I say aloud. "Look, I'm doing it. I'm all right; I'm okay." It's like a school cheer. I sing the ABC song loudly. When I step out I am exhausted, but triumphant. Over a *shower*. Imagine.

The rest of the day I try to make no sudden movements, to not bump into things. In the afternoon, I actually go the hospital to visit a friend who is seriously ill. In the evening I attend sign language class and pass for normal.

But here, tonight, back at what should be my safe place, I feel the fear stalking me. It is at the periphery of my vision; just beyond the light of my campfire it crouches. I get into bed, I turn out the light. Beside my bed I have a shotgun loaded with Valium.

After that episode my fear continued throughout the week. I was afraid of taking my morning shower. I felt the threat of an impending attack constantly. Humbled and ashamed, I called Rick for an appointment. It was the middle of July.

"It's back," Rick said, without equivocation, "for no explainable reason. So let's treat it now." I cried profusely. I'd thought I was cured. All that I had gone through, all the work I had done for the past two years seemed lost, vanished into some kind of black hole where the panic monster lived.

Rick let me choose the form my treatment would take. I decided to start with the Pamelor at half my old dose. I was adamant about not wanting to take Xanax, since I had just spent six months prying that monkey off my back. After two weeks of the Pamelor I was still feeling edgy and nervous. Rick was away on vacation. One night I dreamed I spoke with Rick. He said: "Your body is craving a little more medication. Take an extra pill every other night." And in the dream I smiled and said, "You're right," and then Rick's face turned into a large handmade pottery mug in soothing shades of blue and terra cotta.

So I called Rick's backup, told him the problem, omitted the dream. He said, "Sure, increase the Pamelor every other night. It can't hurt." I did. I believe in dreams, and in second opinions.

When Rick returned we raised the Pamelor to 50mg. nightly. After ten days on this amount, I still was having trouble adjusting. Sometimes I trembled; at times my vision was distorted. One night I was afraid to go to bed because I was convinced I would die in my sleep. On the job I had to have a routine physical which included an EKG. I was all hooked up and resting comfortably until the machine came on. Instantly I was terrified and had the oddest sensation that the machine actually was pulling some kind of energy from my body, or reversing my polarity, or stealing my soul. I know these are illogical thoughts. But the feeling was real.

I told the technician to get those leads off my body, and I helped. Her wide-eyed silence spoke volumes. I couldn't help it. If I wanted to keep on living, I had to get off that table.

My EKG came out "borderline normal." The story of my life. I took a copy of the strip to Rick and showed him a picture of a panic attack.

By now we knew the Pamelor was not sufficient, and the only way was up because of my stubbornness over the Xanax. I agreed to raise it one more time 75mg., although I had never gone above 50 and was nervous about taking this amount. Something in me whispered that my body couldn't handle this level. But I was determined to try.

I gave it my best shot, after three weeks of this I went to Rick's office, burst into tears, and said, "I want my life back! I can't do this anymore." Rick knew it was coming; he just knew it had to come from me. We dropped the Pamelor back to 50mg. and I added the Xanax.

With the first tablet the clouds parted, the birds sang, the snail crawled back on the thorn. I could've kicked myself for being so hardheaded about the Xanax. It was the twenty-second of October, 1991.

November and December were tough months. I learned that a dear friend from college had died suddenly, and I found out too late to attend a service. I cried bitterly for lost youth, for Jack. And we had to have our fifteen-year-old dog put to sleep. He was loving and loyal, and trusting to the end. I sat on the floor and cradled his head while the vet gave him the injection. It took about four seconds for him to become dead weight in my arms, and without so much as a whimper. Is this how you know you're a grownup?

Rufus: 1977-1992

Let's talk about patience here, with yourself, with your condition. By mid-December, my body had adjusted pretty well to the medicine. I thought I'd coast for a little while, let the medicine do the work. You know: "Better Living Through Chemistry."

Anyway, Maxey and I had been Christmas shopping, rushing all over town in a buying frenzy. I had checked out several perfumes, and even had a tissue doused with one in my pocket to see how it performed over time. I was driving home. Halfway there I pulled up to a stop sign and immediately lost my breath. I felt my throat closing up. My chest and neck flushed a deep red.

I told Maxey I was having an attack, asked him to get me a Xanax since I was due for a dose anyway. I dry-swallowed it, and you know that's next to impossible, bitter as they are. I tried to keep breathing. He told me to pull over and let him drive, but I refused. I had to keep driving so I would be forced to concentrate on something outside myself. I though I was going into shock, that a delayed reaction from the perfume was killing me. Honestly. It's not easy to say. And I'm sure Maxey was completely at ease with me behind the wheel, gasping for air, saying I was going to pass out while flooring the accelerator.

Fifteen minutes later we reached the house. I was still frantic. Maxey was upset because 1) he felt helpless and 2) is as sick of this disease as I am and 3) thought I had overheated the engine. And not necessarily in that order. He cooked his own supper and I went to the bedroom to cry. Pure marital bliss.

The crisis passed, but the tail end of the fear hung around all night. The next morning I was tense and uneasy, and everything I did required a huge effort; raising my arms to wash my hair; packing for the trip to Knoxville we were to make that day. I knew I had to get straight before I left home. So I called Rick, told him the sequence of events. "What is your fear?" he said. "That I will stop breathing," I said. "Good!" he said. "Let's deal with that." And he described the chemistry of perfume, and said that by design it produces a flushing sensation, which I suddenly noticed and multiplied tenfold into an attack. He said the anxiety continued because I still believed a reaction was imminent. He said reasonable things. He said a reaction now was virtually impossible, but the key was in whether I believed him, though my voice quivered. I would've clapped my hands for Tinkerbell if I had thought it would help.

---

Rick's words dissipated the fear. I was fine on the trip, had no more close calls. But here's the point, and I think I've made it before, and if I haven't, I've been remiss. There is no miracle cure. I knew the conditions were right for an attack; red flags were everywhere. But when it came, I wasn't prepared. I let it get ahead of me, so far along that my judgment alone was not powerful enough to stop it. I ended up going to the expert, who told me again what I already knew but can't seem to believe. I've been giving advice that I forgot to take myself. I could've let Maxey drive while I mentally charted the time, location, feelings, and all the rest. I could've listed all the causes for the attack. I could've remembered that the medication is not designed to prevent all attacks all the time. I could've reminded Maxey that I needed his support, and that his frustration only serves to make me feel more guilty, and alone, and frightened. I could've read over my list of affirmations which I have not shared with you yet but will in just a moment because it is invaluable to me. There are lots of things I could have done besides clutch my throat and tingle.

So, about patience: I was fresh out. I thought I was on Easy Street right up until the Mack Truck flattened me. I want the panic disorder to go away now, and never return. I want to eat chocolate. I want a Coke. I want not to be different from others in a way that makes me appear weak, or fragile, or hysterical. I need to be more patient with myself, and remember that most of the time I can control these outbreaks. Pretending I don't have this will not stop the attacks; it will guarantee them.

Here is the list of affirmations I mentioned earlier. I got this from the AIA newsletter and I have found it very reassuring. I carry a copy with me always.

I wish I could credit the author, but thank you, whoever you are. I'll put a copy in the Appendix for you to tear out and keep if you want to.

## Things To Remember When You're Panicking

1. It does not matter if you feel frightened, bewildered, unreal, unsteady. These feelings are nothing more than an exaggeration of the bodily reactions to stress.

2. Just because you have these sensations doesn't mean you are sick. These feelings are just unpleasant and frightening, not dangerous. Nothing worse will happen to you.

3. Let your feelings come. They've been in charge of you. You've been pumping them up and making them more acute. Don't run away as you breathe it out, let go. Keep trying. Stay there almost as if you were floating in space. Don't fight the feeling of panic. Accept it. You can do it.

4. Try to make yourself as comfortable as possible without escaping. If you're on a street, lean against a post or a stone wall. If you are in a department store, find a quiet counter or corner. If you are in a car, pull over to the side of the road. Do not jump into a cab and go home in fear.

5. Stop adding to your panic with frightening thoughts about what is happening and where it might lead. Don't indulge in self-pity

or think, "Why can't I be like other people? Why do I have to go through all this?" Just accept what is happening to you. If you do this, what you fear will not happen to you.

6. Think about what is really happening to your body at this moment. Do not think "Something terrible is going to happen. I must get out." Repeat to yourself, "I will not fall, faint, die or lose control."

7. Now wait and give the fear time to pass. Do not run away. Others have found the strength and you will too. Notice that as you stop adding the frightening thoughts to your panic, the fear starts to fade away by itself.

8. This is your opportunity to practice. Think of it that way. Even if you feel isolated in space, one of these days you will not feel that way. Sometime soon you will be able to go through the panic and say "I DID IT." Once you say this, you will have gone a long way toward conquering fear. Think about the progress you have already made. You are in a situation, so practice!

9. Try to distract yourself from what is going on inside you. Look at your surroundings. See other people on the street or otherwise around you. They are with you, not against you.

10. When your panic subsides, let your body go loose, take a deep breath, and go on with your day. Remember, each time you cope with a panic, you reduce your fear.

A word here about fear. Most people think they know fear. You jumped when Glenn Close rose from the bathtub, knife in hand, in "Fatal Attraction." You hear a noise downstairs in the night and your heart starts suddenly. You have to give a speech and your mouth gets dry. Have you ever been deafened by the roar of your blood in your ears? Have you heard the lid slam shut on your coffin? Have you counted your heartbeats without even having to use your hands? Or felt your senses shut down, one by one, until you are certain you will disappear? This is fear. This is the disease that manifests itself, not through fever and chills, or rash, or boils, but through total, irrational fear.

---

Courage has nothing to do with being unafraid. It has everything to do with being terrified, and doing what you need to do anyway. We are the bravest people I know.

---

It's Groundhog Day today, my sister's birthday. It is bright and sunny. I have resumed my sessions with Denise, the Cognitive Therapist, and in my head I refer to them as Remedial Butt-Kicking 101, or Reasonable Lessons. We try to separate irrational fears from reality, or at least the general consensus of reality, the so-called "collective hunch." Denise gives me assignments. One is to list my fears. Another is to make two lists: one of those who accept my disorder, one of those who do not. These are short lists. Most people have no idea I have suffered in any way from panic disorder, although in the past couple of years I have become a little more open about it. The responses are sometimes laughable, like the guy who turned to me in the jam-packed elevator and whispered "You're not going to have one of those *things* are you?" I should have told him I had Tourette's Syndrome.

But by far the most common response is surprise, because they say I look so relaxed, so at ease in the world. Science and skill. Years of practice. We are too good at not getting caught.

Anyway, Denise gives me another assignment: to do something slightly unacceptable, to begin to break my need for others' approval. In theory, if I can become confident of my own judgment, there will be less room for fear. I give it serious thought. Problem is, I already think most of the things I do are slightly unacceptable, at least where I live, and probably in Anytown, USA. Denise herself described me as having "non-mainstream ideas" just because I told her I think part of us leaves our body while we sleep and travels around a bit. Big deal. A television set is more a mystery to me than that.

So here's my quandary: We don't have children and I kept my maiden name. I am a hair's breadth from becoming known as the Crazy Cat Lady of Stratton Lake. What else is left?

My lessons are neverending. A spider bit me on the inside of my upper arm. I can see two tiny holes, like a vampire mark. It frightened me. Denise had to point out to me that this was a *normal* fear, that most people would be frightened by this. Oh. I hadn't considered that I might be having a *normal* reaction. So much to learn. Where is the handbook?

# Chapter 9

I'm putting most of the straight-up advice here in one place, either for easy reference, or so you can avoid it if you like. I've learned a lot since the days that Ava asked me if she would die today, and I am happy to share those things with you. Most I learned through reading, talking with others, and my own experiences. Maybe the most important thing, as I said before, is patience. With myself first, then with others.

Here we go:

1. If you're on medication, take it as it is prescribed for you. Make friends with the medicine and don't fear it. *Never* cut it back or raise it on your own. Always talk this over with your doctor first.

2. Avoid caffeine and alcohol. The panic monster thrives on these things. And yes, unfortunately, this includes chocolate. If you are on medication, this means *total abstinence* from drinking.

3. Be careful of any other medicines you might take, either prescribed or over-the-counter stuff. Many antihistamines contain caffeine; some cough syrups have sedatives in them. In general, I've found that we tend to undermedicate ourselves out of fear of a drug reaction. A common shared fantasy involves throats swelling closed and hearts shutting down. We are a far cry from the *Valley of the Dolls* rejects others might imagine us to be.

4. Exercise, like aerobics, is great. I started taking a class two years ago just to prove to myself that my heart could beat that fast and still be okay. It's worked. As a bonus, my cholesterol has dropped nearly twenty points and I didn't even change my diet.

5. Don't go for long periods without eating. We need food at regular intervals, more so than other people. And don't shove a lot of sugary processed foods in there either. On days when I'm feeling anxious, I try to eat foods like bananas, oatmeal, baked potatoes, and toast. I try to limit red meat, but on a real bad day I can go down to Stratton's

Dairy Dip. The ribeye steak sandwich will not only ground you, it will flat nail your feet to the floor.

6. If you are using the so-called "recreational" drugs (marijuana, cocaine, uppers, downers, movers, and shakers) you are playing Russian Roulette with all the chambers loaded. Please call and let me know when you will be at large, so I won't be. I have read that the severity of a panic attack while on drugs has *many times* the strength of the average attack. Could you survive that?

7. Stop doing things you hate. This is not as easy as it sounds, and far more important than it appears. Persist, and you will find a way.

8. Listen to your body. If it tells you it's tired, get some rest. It has no reason to lie to you. Don't try to control it all the time. Let it do its job, which is to keep you living. It's much better at it than you are.


Okay. So you do all this stuff, make these tremendous sacrifices like giving up chocolate (I really mean it), and still you get an attack. Here are some defensive tactics you can use:

1. If you're in a car, turn the radio up real loud. Sing along with the music. Singing helps regulate your breathing.

2. Take out your affirmation sheet ("It does not matter if you...etc.") and read it, out loud if you can.

3. Eat some heavy, comforting food like potatoes or a vanilla milkshake. The digestive process will slow you down. If your heart is beating rapidly, drink some ice water. This will help slow it down. It's been proven with fish. Don't ask me to elaborate.

4. Score the attack on a scale of one to ten. Use your chart to write out the situation, feelings, thoughts, etc. This helps put some distance between you and the monster.

5. Unless you're driving, *make* yourself move around. Huddling in the corner is the worst thing you can do. Walk. Hit the bed with a pillow. Anything will discharge the pent-up energy.

6. Keep a mental checklist of possible causes and run through it. Did I get enough sleep/food? Is it time for me to ovulate or start my period? (Attacks can increase during these times.) Is something upsetting going on at work or at home I'm trying to avoid? Often, finding the cause can derail the fear if you can just ferret it out.

7. Call someone you trust, someone you know will be reasonable and supportive, who can remind you that this

is only a panic attack and nothing worse (and yes, there *are* worse things, just not at this moment).

8. Do *not* fall prey to that old cure of breathing into a paper bag to stop hyperventilation. Breathing in a bag builds up carbon dioxide, which has been shown to actually bring on panic attacks. You know how we hate crowded, tight spaces like theater lobbies? I know it's partly claustrophobia, but I have this sneaking suspicion that in a crowd like that a lot of carbon dioxide is being generated. So whenever possible, avoid bags and crowds.

I warned you that this was the advice chapter. In this section I want to address all the husbands and wives, and parents and children, and significant and not-so-significant others of those who have panic disorder. What's a body to do, you say as one. If I tell her to get over it and fix the dinner or pick up the kids herself, I'm insensitive. If I respond to the irrational fears with concern, I'm fueling the fire. True, both. You have my deepest sympathy. Life at your house is complicated. You spend half your time berating yourself because you can't fix what's wrong, and the other half silently seething with anger because it's interfering with the life you have planned. Neither is productive. Here are some things you can do to help everybody along.

*Educate yourself* about this disorder. Look in the bookstores. Read the literature. If you need to, go along to talk to whoever your panicked person is seeing professionally. Ask questions. Look for free seminars put on by hospitals or mental health centers about panic disorder. Information is everywhere.

*Be supportive* as much as you can. When symptoms arise, when she shakes you awake in the dead of night claiming she's blind in one eye, take a moment to collect yourself. Then *you* be the cognitive therapist. Reason with her. Examine her eye and pronounce it healthy (assuming it is). *Do not* jump out of bed, pull on sweatpants, and declare you're taking her to the nearest emergency room. This is the time to say (while holding her, if you're not too disoriented): "This is just a panic attack. There is nothing wrong with your eye. This will pass." Staying calm and composed helps her tremendously. And repeat the above as often as needed. If you can actually pinpoint the underlying cause of the attack, the duck comes down and gives you a hundred dollars.

Remember, she simultaneously is overwhelmed with terror and humiliated beyond belief. There is a part of her that knows she has not suddenly been stricken blind, but that part simply cannot fight its way to the forefront. The cattle are stampeding. Climb a tree and hold on until they pass. Don't try to shame her out of her fear. It will only serve to make her feel more ashamed and guilty, and make you look like a heartless worm — not your best side.

It *is* infuriating. This disease can level a marriage, separate families, destroy all kinds of relationships. It's kind of like living with an alcoholic: you never know what to expect. Will you be able to go to dinner with friends, or will she have an attack that keeps you at home? Do you dare plan a trip longer than the distance to the nearest emergency room? Will you ever see the ocean again? And where, oh where, is the fun-loving, capable, independent woman you used to know? You grieve for the life you once knew, and for the one you planned, and curse the disease. So does she. So does she.

It's a fine line you need to walk here. You can show concern, but not fear. You can remind her it's nothing more serious than a panic attack, but not in a disparaging way. I know this is a tall order. I realize there will be days when you want to say, "I have needs too; what about *my* needs?" And that should be said. You must talk about her fears and feelings, but you must share your own as well. There's a balance that is necessary to maintain; and strike me dead if I use the word *communicate*, but you both have to talk and you both have to listen. It will help. The better you understand what's going on, the more helpful, and less resentful, you can be. This is not a disease we have chosen. We cannot necessarily make its symptoms stop, but we can choose how we respond to those symptoms. And you can help tremendously by supporting the right choice.

Please, please don't condemn the treatment plan. This is the fastest, deadliest form of sabotage. We have had to learn to put our faith, and yes, our lives, into someone else's hands and trust that the plan we have chosen together will work. Don't say things like Xanax is more addictive than heroin or you "know someone" that anything negative happened to while in treatment. This is our lifeline. Don't make us doubt its tensile strength. If the treatment plan sounds too farfetched, or you really believe it's damaging in some way, talk to the person in charge and express your concerns. (Don't do this without permission from the one in treatment first. *That* would be bad form.) Find out the rationale. You may learn something. This is a complicated condition, with many twists and turns and dead ends, and it takes an expert to maneuver through this rat's maze. And at the end, instead of the cheese, you just might get your life back.

Let me mention a little about the literature. My exploration has been woefully inadequate, but for a good reason: I was afraid I would be so intimidated by the books that I would not be able to write one of my own. Luckily, early on I found the book *The Anxiety Disease* by David Sheehan, M.D. I was so excited I gave it to Sandra immediately and told her as my best friend she had a responsibility to read it. It was a very important book for me. I no longer felt crazy and alone.

The author is excellent at explaining the mechanics and treatment of the disease. But for sheer comfort and reassurance, pick up Dr. Claire Weekes' book *Hope and Help For Your Nerves.* You'll feel as though your grandmother just wrapped you in a quilt and handed you a nice cup of tea. This woman is a treasure. *Peace From Nervous Suffering* is another of her books. Check these two out.

On the other side, *The Good News About Panic, Anxiety and Phobias* by Mark Gold, M.D., turned out to be not such good news for me. This is a great book for diagnosticians, because it details every single medical condition that can mimic panic disorder. Since I was already diagnosed, it simply gave me scores of new diseases I hadn't even dreamed I might have, and made me question my diagnosis. What if it really *is* my thyroid, or schizophrenia, or mercury poisoning? Case in point: Dr. Gold begins the book with the story of a man who was treated for years for panic disorder, only to discover he was suffering from diabetes. Great. At the very least I need to have confidence that I have been diagnosed correctly. I mean if I can't trust my panic, what *can* I trust?

I am told there are several good books out there to help you. Go and investigate. Learn all you can. Make your own decisions about what works best for you. Then do it.

It's odd; giving all this advice arouses the panic monster. Even in his sleep he groans and rolls heavily onto his side. I tiptoe out of this chapter. I've preached enough anyway.

# Chapter 10

Springtime, 1993. I'd been on my second round of medication for almost a year. Rick and I were meeting once a month for a thirty-minute chat about the state of my state (or the '60s song: to see what condition my condition was in). Usually, I didn't have much news. My symptoms were controlled, and I wasn't even considering getting off the medicine any time soon after my last experience with rebound.

So how could I stir things up? How about *changing* medication? Even though the Pamelor was suppressing the panic, I was really tired of the side effects—the dry mouth, the sluggish digestive system, blood pressure dropping when I stood up too quickly, the frequent flushing of my skin. I took it to Rick: What about Zoloft? I queried. Rick replied: I've been waiting for you to ask, and smiled. He understands better than most that you can't push the river. Not with the Panic People.

So we worked out a schedule to begin the tradeoff from Pamelor to Zoloft. I figured it would take about a week. Right. Turns out Zoloft has some interesting side effects of its own: nausea, diarrhea, headache, insomnia. In all the places Pamelor slows down, Zoloft speeds up. My body was in a quandary, caught between conflicting signals. And in the midst of this confusion, Rick left town for a convention. So in his absence, I called his colleague. He told me to raise the Xanax, but unfortunately also told me Zoloft was not a drug he prescribed. Oops. My confidence slipped another 20%. And upcoming was a week's vacation in Colorado. Luckily, Rick arrived home the night before we left, and told me to add in the reduced dose of Pamelor. This would help counteract the insomnia and diarrhea.

So once again Rick got the White Knight Award for saving the day. My vacation would have been a disaster had I not taken the Pamelor. It did serve as a counterbalance to the Zoloft, and I was able to ride horses and trains and go down into mines, just like in the Immodium AD commercials.

My system very gradually adjusted to the Zoloft, although I continued a small dose of Pamelor at night. It helps the Xanax work better. I still have to watch my diet to maintain my weight because my digestive system is so outrageously efficient. People hate me for this. Sometimes when they ask me how I stay so thin I just tell them I have worms. It stops the questions. The good news about Zoloft is it really works to quell the panic. Less delightful is the prospect of my skirt falling off any second. I try to maintain perspective and not dwell on the last time I was too thin: the oh-so-effective Death and Depression Diet Plan.

And so I have reached a truce with my body: we take Zoloft in the morning, Xanax through the day, and a tiny dose of Pamelor at night. I've adjusted, physically and egotistically, to taking three medications a day instead of two. I have no more illusions about being medicine-free for the rest of my life. I do believe I will have time periods—months, or even years—when I can manage without it, but I anticipate periodically needing drug treatment. This is not a negative thought. It is a realistic one. It does not mean I have lost hope, or have become helplessly dependent on medication. It is more like having sense enough to use a cast when your arm is broken. We all know the cast does not cause the healing; it only *allows* the healing to occur. This is the way I see the medicine. It lets us mend for a little while. Cruise control.

Nowadays I don't have the classic panic attacks. I have moments when a wave will rise in me, but it subsides before it crashes on the shoreline. I confess I still wait for the sound.

I pretty much do what I need to do to stay well. I like my work. I try to keep things simple. When I am faced with something really upsetting or panic-provoking, like the recent deaths of two friends, I look at the fear, feel it, and go on. It sounds easy. It's taken me years to learn how to do that. I have fears about this book. What if no one will publish it? What if someone *does* publish it? I can't be guided by fear in either direction. You must have faith for any of this to work—in yourself, in your treatment, in God. And not in that order.

Medicine is an imperfect science. Life is a mess, all bumpy and uneven, and on bad days I skip the evening news. I am so lucky I found Rick, that I have a wonderful loving family and friends who will go the last mile with me, no questions asked, and that I found weapons and the strength to fight the overwhelming terror that can rob you of your life.

This book most certainly is not the answer for you. I hope it will be a starting place, a beginning, a candle in the window. I want you to know that you are not crazy, and that you are not alone. Most of all I want you to understand that what is happening to you is not your fault. You are not being punished for some past sin. You need some support, some advice, maybe some medicine, and lots of patience. Do the exercises. Use the list of affirmations. Learn all you can. Knowledge may not be power, but it will give you some snappy comebacks to those who would be less than understanding of this condition.

———

Just the other day I was walking to my car after work, head down, when suddenly red spots appeared before my eyes. Oh no, I thought, What if — and then I looked up and saw the branches above me, heavy-laden with red berries. I laughed.

Got you last, said the Panic Monster, scampering away.

# *Appendix*

I. Anatomy of an Attack

II. Things to Remember When You're Panicking

III. Denise's Lists

IV. Notes and Resources

# I. ANATOMY OF AN ATTACK

Date:                          Time:

Location:


Feelings:


Thoughts:


Alternatives:


Probable Causes:


140

# II. THINGS TO REMEMBER WHEN YOU'RE PANICKING

1. It does not matter if you feel frightened, bewildered, unreal, unsteady. These feelings are nothing more than an exaggeration of the bodily reactions to stress.

2. Just because you have these sensations doesn't mean you are sick. These feelings are just unpleasant and frightening, not dangerous. Nothing worse will happen to you.

3. Let your feelings come. They've been in charge of you. You've been pumping them up and making them more acute. Don't run away as you breathe it out, let go. Keep trying. Stay there almost as if you were floating in space. Don't fight the feeling of panic. Accept it. You can do it.

4. Try to make yourself as comfortable as possible without escaping. If you're on a street, lean against a post or a stone wall. If you are in a department store, find a quiet counter or corner. If you are in a car, pull over to the side of the road. Do not jump into a cab and go home in fear.

5. Stop adding to your panic with frightening thoughts about what is happening and where it might lead. Don't indulge in self-pity or think, "Why can't I be like other people? Why do I have to go through all this?" Just accept what is happening to you. If you do this, what you fear will not happen to you.

6. Think about what is really happening to your body at this moment. Do not think "Something terrible is going to happen. I must get out." Repeat to yourself, "I will not fall, faint, die or lose control."

7. Now wait and give the fear time to pass. Do not run away. Others have found the strength and you will too. Notice that as you stop adding the frightening thoughts to your panic, the fear starts to fade away by itself.

8. This is your opportunity to practice. Think of it that way. Even if you feel isolated in space, one of these days you will not feel that way. Sometime soon you will be able to go through the panic and say "I DID IT." Once you say this, you will have gone a long way toward conquering fear. Think about the progress you have already made. You are in a situation, so practice!

9. Try to distract yourself from what is going on inside you. Look at your surroundings. See other people on the street or otherwise around you. They are with you, not against you.

10. When your panic subsides, let your body go loose, take a deep breath, and go on with your day. Remember, each time you cope with a panic, you reduce your fear.

# III. DENISE'S LISTS

*People who accept me
  with panic disorder

People who do not accept
me with panic disorder

_____          _____

_____          _____

_____          _____

_____          _____

_____          _____

_____          _____

_____          _____

_____          _____

_____          _____

_____          _____

_____          _____

*which list has your own name?

# NOTES

1. Words by Charles Bates, Bob Bigelow, Jack Yellin, music by Milton Ager, "Hard-Hearted Hannah", 1929.

2. Edna St. Vincent Millay, "The Merry Maid", *Collected Poems*. Camp Hill, PA: Harper Collins Publishers, Inc., 1990, p. 145.

3. Walt Kelly, *Pogo*: *We Have Met the Enemy and He Is Us*. New York: Simon and Schuster, 1972.

4. Robert Frost, "Bereft", *Robert Frost's Poems*. New York: Pocketbooks, a division of Simon and Schuster, 1973, p. 175.

## RESOURCES

Agoraphobics in Action, Inc. (newsletter), Antioch, TN, (615) 831-2383.

Freedom from Fear, 308 Seaview Avenue, Staten Island, NY, 10305.

National Center for the Treatment of Phobias, Anxiety, and Depression, 1755 S. Street, NW, Washington, D.C., 20009.

National Council of Community Mental Health Centers, 12300 Twinbrook Parkway, Suite 320, Rockville, MD 20852.

Anxiety Disorders Association of America, 6000 Executive Blvd., Rockville, MD 20852-3801, (301) 231-9350.

BOOKS & TAPES FROM

# Thom Rutledge Publishing

|  | Quantity | Total |
|---|---|---|

## Life with the Panic Monster .... $9.95    ___    $ ___
by Evelyn Barkley Stewart

*Books & Tapes by Thom Rutledge:*

BOOKS

## SIMPLE TRUTH . . . . . . . . . . . . . . . $8.95    ___    $ ___
*A book for readers serious about learning self-compassion.*
*Includes ten (10) of Thom's creative therapeutic exercises.*

## IF I WERE THEY . . . . . . . . . . . . . . $6.95    ___    $ ___
*A handbook of self-helpful wisdom with a dash of humor.*
*Makes an attractive and thoughtful gift.*

TAPES

## PRACTICE MAKES PRACTICE . . . $9.95    ___    $ ___
*Information-packed cassette will guide you from destructive*
*self-criticism toward essential self-compassion. Includes 3 exercises.*

## DEFINING THE INNER CHILD . . . $9.95    ___    $ ___
*An informal and intelligent introduction to the healing metaphor*
*so widely used, it has entered our cultural mainstream.*

In TN, add 8.25% sales tax . . . . . . . . . . . . . . . . . . . . . . . . . . . . .$ ___

Postage & Handling: $3.00 per order . . . . . . . . . . . . . . . . . . . $ __3.00__

**A personal check/money order is enclosed in the amount of . . . $ ___**

*SHIPPING ADDRESS:*

| NAME | PHONE    / |
|---|---|
| STREET | APT# |
| CITY | STATE          ZIP |

Thom Rutledge Publishing  ♦  331 22nd Ave N, Suite One  ♦  Nashville, TN  37203
Call (615) 327-3423 to request a FREE BROCHURE
**TO ORDER BY CREDIT CARD:  1-800-532-4769**